T4-AHF-726

Letters of
Brunswick and Hessian Officers
During the American Revolution

A Da Capo Press Reprint Series

THE ERA OF THE AMERICAN REVOLUTION

GENERAL EDITOR: LEONARD W. LEVY

Brandeis University

Letters of
Brunswick and Hessian Officers
During the American Revolution

Translated by
WILLIAM L. STONE

DA CAPO PRESS · NEW YORK · 1970

081230S'

~~100117~~

A Da Capo Press Reprint Edition

This Da Capo Press edition of
Letters of Brunswick and Hessian Officers During the American Revolution
is an unabridged republication of the first edition
published in Albany, New York, in 1891

Library of Congress Catalog Card Number 76-112706

SBN 306-71919-3

Published by Da Capo Press
A Division of Plenum Publishing Corporation
227 West 17th Street, New York, N.Y. 10011
All Rights Reserved

Manufactured in the United States of America

Letters of
Brunswick and Hessian Officers
During the American Revolution

SCHLÖZER.

LETTERS

OF

BRUNSWICK AND HESSIAN OFFICERS

DURING THE

AMERICAN REVOLUTION.

TRANSLATED BY

WILLIAM L. STONE,

Author of " The Life and Times of Sir William Johnson, Bart.," " Memoirs of General and Madame Riedesel," " History of New York City," " Life and Writings of Col. William L. Stone," " Sir John Johnson's Orderly Book," etc., etc.

(ASSISTED BY AUGUST HUND.)

" Far from me and from my friends be such frigid philosophy as may conduct us indifferent and unmoved over any ground which has been dignified by wisdom, bravery, or virtue. That man is little to be envied whose patriotism would not gain force upon the plain of Marathon, or whose piety would not grow warmer among the ruins of Iona." —*Dr. Johnson, in his " Tour of the Hebrides."*

ALBANY, N. Y.

JOEL MUNSELL'S SONS, PUBLISHERS.

1891.

TO THE MEMORY

OF THE LATE

PARKER HANDY,

THE EMINENT BANKER,

OF

NEW YORK CITY,

WHOSE PATRIOTIC SERVICES, DURING THE LATE CIVIL WAR, STRENGTHENED

THE CREDIT OF THE GOVERNMENT, AND THUS CONTRIBUTED TO

PRESERVE THE REPUBLIC WHICH THE BLOOD OF

OUR FOREFATHERS HAD ESTABLISHED,

This Volume

IS AFFECTIONATELY INSCRIBED

BY

THE TRANSLATOR.

PREFACE.

In 1776, Professor August Ludwig Schlözer, of the University of Göttingen, established a monthly magazine called "Schlözer's Letter Exchange," having for one of its objects the publication of private letters written by officers to their relatives and friends in Germany, from those portions of the world then engaged in war. This publication was continued through the year 1782, and consequently contains many letters of the most interesting character from Hessian and Brunswick military men who were serving on the British side during the Revolutionary War; and also one from Baron Steuben on his first arrival in America, giving a detailed account of his reception by the authorities at Portsmouth, N. H., and later by Washington, the military formation of the American troops, and his successful efforts in disciplining the Continental army. These letters are from Staunton, Va. (whither a portion of the "Convention Troops" were sent), Philadelphia, Savannah, New-Port, Cambridge, Boston, New York, Brookland (Brooklyn), different parts of New England, and Canada. They contain much new and valuable information regarding the habits and customs of the inhabitants of the places whence they were written; minute descriptions of different personages, such as Gates, Hancock, Carleton, St. Luc, and others; and also the best account extant of the march of the "Convention Troops" from Saratoga through New-England to Cambridge. The letter from New-England contains a graphic description of the costumes and general appearance of the Continentals and militia,—to which the attention of the reader is especially called,—and a narrative of the Battles of Saratoga by an eye-witness, which is by far the best we have yet had; also, a very realistic account of the trial of Major Henley and the part taken in it by Burgoyne—the only one written from a German standpoint.

This work was first brought to my notice by Mr. Edward J. Lowell, the author of the "Hessians in the American Revolution." "I do not think," writes Mr. Lowell, "of any printed collection concerning the Revolution which so well deserves to be translated. The correspondent with Burgoyne's army was an observant and lively writer." Through the kindness of Fräulien Agnes Sack, of Brunswick, Germany, I procured a set of the first edition of this rare publication, and now present to the reader, in an English dress, those letters which relate to our Revolution.

As I said in my Preface to *Pausch's Journal*, there are two ways of translating. One is to paraphrase the original; the other is to give the text literally. The first method admits of an elegant rendering by which the different shades of an author's meaning are often sacrificed to beauty of diction: the second, at the expense of style, aims to give clearly the writer's ideas. This last is the plan I have adopted in this translation, believing that the reader would prefer to know just what the correspondents intended to convey.

Among those who have assisted me by their counsel and suggestions, I have particularly to mention and thank Dr. Kingsford, author of the latest history of Canada; Mr. Fred. C. Würtele, Librarian of the Quebec Historical Society; Mr. J. G. Rosengarten, the author of the "German Soldier in the Wars of the United States;" Professor Carl Meyer, of Rutgers College; Mr. S. O. Lee, of Huntington, L. I.; and Mr. Bauman L. Belden, of Elizabeth, N. J. Mr. August Hund, an accomplished scholar and himself a German, has also rendered so much aid in this translation, that I have thought it only just to associate his name with mine on the title-page. The annotations, of course, are my own.

Believing, moreover, that it would afford pleasure to my subscribers, I have given, by way of introduction, a sketch of Schlözer—the materials for which have been gathered from the "Life of August Ludwig Schlözer," written by his eldest son, Christian von Schlözer, and published at Leipsic, in 1828. For the use of this work, which, long out of print, is seldom if ever met with, I am again indebted to the courtesy of my friend Mr. Edward J. Lowell.

WILLIAM L. STONE.

JERSEY CITY HEIGHTS, June, 1891.

TABLE OF CONTENTS.

0812308

100117

APPENDIX.

SKETCH OF SCHLÖZER.

AUGUST LUDWIG SCHLÖZER was, perhaps, one of the most distinguished scholars and historians of his time. His father was a country clergyman at Yaggstadt, a village in Hohenlohe-Kirchberg, where his only son, the subject of the present sketch, was born, July 5th, 1735. His father dying when he was five years old, his education was taken in charge by his grandfather, who sent him to school at Langenburg. He was an exceedingly precocious lad, being considered what is now termed an "infant prodigy," and at the age of twelve years was an accomplished Latin scholar. From Langenburg he went to Wertheim, residing in the family of his eldest sister, the wife of the pastor of the town, Schulz (father of the celebrated Oriental scholar of that name), until the autumn of 1751 ; when, at the age of sixteen, he entered the University of Wittenberg, famous not only for its own sake, but for having been the place at which, in

1517, the Reformation under Martin Luther took its
rise.   Here he remained until the spring of 1754—
taking, meanwhile, high rank as a debater—when he
went to the University of Göttingen, and pursued his
studies at that seat of learning until the following
year, when he engaged himself as a teacher at Stock-
holm.   Two years afterward he removed to Upsala
in order to take advantage of the valuable library at
that celebrated university ; and here he seems to have
completed his collegiate course.   Nor, had he long
come to maturity when his learning was sought by
various universities of prominence.   During his life-
time he filled successively the chairs of Political Economy and Diplomacy in the Imperial University of
Moscow, Polite Letters and the Fine Arts at St.
Petersburg and Mittau, and Polite Letters at the
University of Göttingen.   He also held at Göttingen
the position of President of the Philosophical Faculty
and Doctor of Laws and Jurisprudence, having been
the first Protestant elected in that university to the
latter honor.   He was also a great traveller ; and his
journeys through Russia, Sweden, Italy, and France
contributed, together with the fame of his scholarly at
tainments, to widen the circle of his acquaintance, and
thus make his name still more known.

   It was while Professor at Göttingen that his *Brief-*

wechsel (from which the letters in this volume are taken) was published—the origin of which was as follows: Having a very extensive acquaintance with men of letters, with whom he was in constant correspondence, he conceived the idea of publishing from time to time a portion of these, so that the valuable news they contained regarding the social, political, and military events then occurring in different parts of the world might be made accessible to the public. A number of educated and talented Hanoverian, Brunswick and Hessian officers, then serving in America, also volunteered to aid him in this work ; and the result was his *Briefwechsel*, at least eight numbers of which were issued yearly. The idea took like wild-fire ; and, within a very short time, the circulation of the magazine had increased to such an extent that even at the very low price at which it was sold, viz., two *gute Groschen* (two cents in our money), it brought its editor an income of three thousand rix-dollars—an income from literature alone which, with the exception of Kotzcbue and Goethe, had seldom been exceeded by any German writer at that time.

Physically, Schlözer was a little above the average height, very thin, and, in the early part of his life, sickly-looking though of an iron constitution,—and his features, notwithstanding his massive brow, repel-

lent, rather than attractive. Morally, he was of an in-
corruptible integrity, of great conscientiousness, very
frank and open, and grateful for any attention. In
temperament, he was, at the same time, both choleric
and melancholy, and two of his salient traits were his
intense loyalty to his government, and his anxiety to
perform faithfully his duties as a citizen. We are
further told that he was a man of great energy and
industry. This will readily be believed when it is
learned that, in addition to his didactic duties, he
found time to write no less than sixty-eight abstruse
and voluminous works, some of which, on history and
political ethics, have, in his own country, still an authoritative value.

Upon his death, which was caused by apoplexy on
the 9th of September 1809, his family were the recipients of many tokens of sympathy, not only from numerous learned and scientific societies of which he was a
member, but from men of high standing, and even
from Royalty itself. One of these marks of respect
was a letter from the Emperor Alexander of Russia,
in which, as a particular tribute to the memory of
Schlözer, he appointed his nephew vice-consul of
Lubeck.

LETTER FROM CANADA, BY A GERMAN STAFF-OFFICER.

BATISCAMP, a Parish in Canada, Nov. 2, 1776.

MY DEAR FRIEND :

The whole of Canada contains but three cities, viz., Quebec, Three Rivers and Montreal—all of which are situated on the St. Lawrence River. All the other European settlements are divided into Parishes or Forts. These Parishes are so numerous that upwards of seven thousand fighting men could be mustered in a stretch of land reaching from *Bec* Island (situated not far from the Gulf of St. Lawrence) to Montreal, and farther south to Lake Champlain.

A Parish is a kind of village composed of houses not placed alongside of each other, but scattered about at 100, 200, and even 600 paces apart—woodlands often intervening between. You will, therefore, readily see that a Parish is generally several leagues in extent.* The main road [highway] invari-

---

* A French league is about two and three-quarter English miles.

ably runs directly into them; and from the fact that the houses are built on both sides of the road, one, in passing, can take in the entire village at a glance ; and should a stream or a river be situated in the rear of a Parish and running toward it, you will probably also find houses built along its banks. The houses are invariably placed side by side along the road; never in the rear of each other. Every *habitant* has his fields, meadows and gardens either in front or at the rear of his house, just as circumstances and the character of the ground will permit ; and he also owns a piece of woodland in the vicinity. Every field and meadow is enclosed by a light fence, which, if necessary, can be shifted about. Whoever has seen the enclosed marshy lands in the neighborhood of Bremen will understand precisely my meaning ; and indeed, take it all in all, Canadian agriculture has much in common with that city. The fallow lands furnish the best of pasture for cattle, and after a certain time, develop into the best of corn-fields.

Until late in the winter, the cattle roam at will either about the enclosures or in the woods, both day and night. Utilizing the manure of cattle is unknown here, and, consequently, the straw-crop is unusually poor. Those fields which are to be planted in the following year are ploughed late in the fall, and remain in that state during the entire winter.

In the spring, the corn-seed is sowed, and then the field is harrowed by three good harrows. Very good wheat is raised in Canada ; also considerable barley and oats ; but summer and winter crops of rye are never cultivated. Peas, tares* and beans are also grown ; and in the gardens you may find white cabbage, white and yellow turnips, potatoes, pumpkins, cucumbers, leeks, onions, parsley, and quite often melons and asparagus. In the vicinity of Montreal winter fruit is good and plentiful. The poorer inhabitants do not bother themselves with the cultivation of fruit-trees, because, in the winter, unless very great care is exercised, a large proportion of them are liable to die. I have eaten here good apples, excellent pears, peaches and apricots ; the latter fruit, however, is exceedingly rare. Hazel- and wall-nuts [walnuts] are not to be found ; but raspberries, and wild strawberries grow abundantly in the woods.

The breed of cattle raised in Canada is excellent. Every *habitant* has his horse, oxen, cows, pigs and sheep ; and once in a while—though very seldom— he keeps goats. The oxen weigh from 300 to 600 pounds each, are very fat, and the flavor of their flesh is excellent. Canada delivered to our army, the current year, several thousand head of cattle, and yet there appears to be no scarcity in this respect. One, too, cannot wish for better milk or butter. Cheese, however, is but seldom made. Each inhabitant has chickens, turkeys and geese in plenty. Tame ducks are not to be seen, but may be found wild in large

---

* A plant more common in Europe than in Canada, and extensively cultivated for fodder.

numbers on the rivers and streams. The same may also be said of pigeons.

Thoughout the whole of Canada neither beer nor brandy is made. Rum is the only liquor manufactured; and the spruce-beer, which is made from the tender sprouts of the spruce-tree, is at first disgustingly sweet, then bitter and with a resinous taste. Wine is not so very dear. A very good so-called red wine (*vin de Bordeaux*)—the only French wine to be had—can be bought at wholesale for from 8 to 10 pence a bottle. Madeira, Port and other kinds of Spanish wine can also be purchased quite cheaply. French white wines, however, as well as Burgundy, Champagne, Rhine, and all French brandies, are largely contraband goods.

In the centre of each Parish are to be found a church and a parsonage; and the leagues are computed from one church to another. The houses of the inhabitants are square and all of the same style of architecture; the only difference being that one, perhaps, may be larger than another. When stone can be had, the walls of the houses are built of that material, and in default of that, of wood; and this, too, notwithstanding the severe cold of the winter months. Indeed, I should say that less than one twentieth of all the houses in Canada are built of stone. I have, as yet, seen no stone-quarries here. Flint, brought from the banks of rivers where it has been deposited from the tops of mountains by the action of frost, is the kind of stone which is used in building. Brick and tiles are unknown in Canada.

The interiors of stone and wooden houses are as like as two peas. The foundation of a wooden house consists of four beams, upon which is placed the scantling. These beams are laid in the form of a square with the corners joined together. Smaller beams are then nailed between the four upright posts, composing the framework of the house ; and the chinks are filled in with moss, small stones, mortar and lime. The outside walls are then covered with lime or with boards, as the case may be ; and, for this reason, such a house (if we except the windows) generally has the appearance of a shed. Sometimes, instead of covering the outer walls with boards, shingles are used, which give the house quite an aristocratic appearance. In the interior, the walls are covered with smoothly planed boards; likewise the ceiling. No lime [i.e. plaster] is put upon the walls as with us at home.

All the partitions of the house are built with wooden boards. For this reason, one will find the three following inconveniences. First : should any one be walking about the rooms, you will hear a slight creaking ; secondly : should any one be walking on the floor overhead, the one underneath would be in momentary expectation of having him drop down upon his head ; and, thirdly : should one talk, every word can be heard, either in the next room or in the kitchen ! Take it all in all, however, the rooms are regularly built and have a well-proportioned height. In order to enter the house, you must mount two or three steps. In every Parish, you will rarely find more than two houses two stories high. Even the houses of the *seigneurs* and rich inhabitants are seldom more than one story in height, and are but a little larger than those of the ordinary inhabitant. The vestibule generally contains the kitchen (similar in character to those of most of French villages) ; and the hearth consists of a large fireplace with two iron andirons capable of holding half of a tree-trunk. The iron cooking-pots are ranged about the fire. The kitchens are so clean that they are used as a "living-room" until the arrival of cold weather. The cooking-utensils, plates, bowls, etc., are of English stone-ware or delft; very rarely of tin. They are put in closets; for large dressers or tables are un-known. Instead, a small table, or the floor, is used-Next to the kitchen is a room generally used as a sleeping-room. Houses containing two rooms are scarce; and when they contain *three* are considered very genteel. The windows extend from the top of the ceiling to a short distance from the floor. They consist of two casements with twelve large square panes fastened on the outside with putty in a wooden frame. Two bolts, one placed above and the other below, are used for closing the windows. When these bolts are withdrawn, the windows always open into the room. Every room has a fireplace. At the beginning of winter the fireplace is walled up ; and a large, square iron stove is placed in the centre of the room, the pipe belonging to it leading into the chimney. As yet, I have seen no stoves with head-pieces.*

---

* Alluding to the stoves in Germany, which are generally ornamented with mythological and classical designs.

In every room one will find at least one bed capable of holding two persons. As a rule, these beds have a large square canopy, fastened to the ceiling, with curtains which are generally drawn up. All bedsteads are square and without posts. The best of them have a bed well filled with straw nearly a foot in thickness, and over which is thrown a nicely stuffed feather-bed. For the head is a bolster nearly a foot in thickness (*rouleau* is the name given them in the inns throughout France). The bed, also, has two linen sheets; and for covering there are four thick woollen blankets. Furthermore, every person receives a pillow a yard long by three quarters wide. You lie perfectly straight in bed; and I have already acquired the art of doing without superfluous bolsters in the future. As soon as you get out of bed, it is made up and covered with a quilt of silesia, calico or wool, with the ends hanging down over the sides. The poorest inhabitant has such a covering for his bed by day; nor, indeed, have I ever seen cleaner beds in any country. In the houses of the poorer people all the beds are placed in one room.

The Canadian is not bothered with unnecessary furniture. Two pine tables, with their necessary accompaniments, eight wooden chairs (never more) with red bottoms and which sometimes have cushions, a few pine closets, and seldom more than one bureau of the same wood, constitute his entire outfit. Sofas, settees, arm-chairs, writing-tables, etc., are unknown. Coffee and tea services of English yellow-ware are common, as are other articles for the table.   I have frequently seen ordinary inhabitants in possession of several dozen of silver spoons, knives and forks, and other silver-ware, although they may not have been quite of the latest style.

Neither will you find any door in the house having a lock, not even in the houses of the rich.   A long iron latch keeps the door closed, a bolt being used to fasten it.   It is but seldom that you will find a water-closet, either in the house or in the yard.   All roofs, even those of churches, are covered with boards or shingles.   The houses, as well as the barns and stables, are free from all fences or stockades.   The stables are built of hewn logs covered with sods, straw, or the bark of the birch ; and I am astonished to find that cattle can survive the winter in these enclosures.

The whole of Canada is ruled by a Governor resid-ing in Quebec.   The present one is Carleton, who is also General of the English Infantry.   He commands the army in Canada, as well as exercises an entire supervision over the military and civil government. The army, as well as the Canadians, love General Carleton dearly—a fact to be attributed to his many noble qualities.   No people ever loved their ruler more than the Canadians do theirs, and this may be said almost without an exception.   The Canadians, as well as the Indians in the vicinity, seem to belong to him body and soul : we are indebted to him for having the Indians (one thousand of whom are in the army) on

our side.* Next to the Governor, there is a Lieutenant-Governor, who, however, has only charge of the
police, the civil service, and all financial matters. The
present Lieutenant-Governor is named Cramahe—also
an upright, disinterested man, and one universally beloved. Under him there are several counselors, or
rather secretaries, to the Government, all of whom are
persons of distinction in this vast territory.

In Quebec is located the chief tribunal for the decision of all matters pertaining to civil and criminal law.
It is made up of native-born Canadians, and has a Chief
Justice, together with advisory counsellors [associate
justices] and assessors. In Montreal there is likewise
a judicial tribunal, which in some respects, however,
ranks below that at Quebec. In the spring both tribu-
nals send judges into all the Parishes of Canada for
the purpose of trying all minor cases, and to see, at the
same time, that the law is properly enforced. The
more important causes are tried before the full tribunal, in which case the litigants must hire counsel who
are to be found in Quebec and Montreal. Should the

---

* Of General Carleton—the ablest general by far who
served in America—General Riedesel, in a letter to his wife,
dated June 8, 1776, gives a peculiar picture. "In order,"
he writes, "to get an idea of his personal appearance, imagine
the Abbé Jerusalem. The figure, face, walk, and sound of
his voice are just like the Abbé's, and had he the black suit
wig, one could not discover the least difference." The Abbé
here mentioned was the tutor of the hereditary prince of
Brunswick, Charles William Ferdinand.

sum involved in a case exceed £500 sterling, an appeal may be made either to the Canadian Government or to his Majesty's Privy Counsellors at London. With the exception of the two above-named cities, no other courts of justice and no other advocates can be found in the whole of Canada. As a rule, two or three Parishes have one regularly appointed notary in common, who draws up contracts, agreements, wills, marriage-settlements etc.

Canada has another peculiar political institution which dates back from the time when the French were its masters. All the Parishes are divided into three districts, each one having a Colonel of Militia at its head. These three Colonels, who reside in Quebec, Three Rivers and Montreal, execute through their subordinates all the commands, notices, etc., of the Government, and collect all of the taxes. These subordinates, who are called Lieutenant-Colonels and Majors of Militia, have, in their turn, charge of several smaller districts, and command the captains of militia.

Each Parish has its Captain of Militia, and, should it be a large one, it may have two. These captains are residents of the Parishes, and have nothing, excepting the office they hold, to distinguish them from their neighbors. They work and clothe themselves the same as the rest of the inhabitants, and receive their positions through election and confirmation of the same by the Colonel. In fact, they occupy about the same rank in the Parishes that our magistrates or mayors do at home. The commands of the Govern-

ment are promulgated by them in the Parishes; they
see to it that they are obeyed; in short, they enforce
the police laws and are held responsible for the behavior
of the inhabitants. In addition to this, they have to
provide quarters for the soldiers that march through
their Parishes, and furnish them with all necessary
transportation. When required by the Generals, they
order out the inhabitants for working purposes, such as
driving, etc., and also furnish the supplies they have
been ordered to procure. They likewise see to it that
the roads and bridges in the several Parishes are kept
in proper repair. They also supervise the forwarding
from Parish to Parish of the letters and military orders
of the different Generals to each other, and are responsible for such documents reaching their proper destination. Under them are two Lieutenants of Police
who assist them in their work, as well as several Sergeants, through whom their orders are delivered to the
inhabitants. These Captains of Militia are held by the
Government to a strict accountability for everything
going on in their several Parishes. Captains who
should prove insubordinate, or should foster rebellious
ideas by designedly refusing to exercise their authority
or otherwise, would be harshly dealt with, even if they
were not punished by death. Such instances have
already occurred. On the other hand, the authority
of these men is sustained in various ways; and those
who are refractory are either executed or put to work
on the fortifications on the frontiers. If a Parish contains a number of rebellious inhabitants, their cattle are

forfeited ; the fire is extinguished on the hearth ; and the roofs of the houses are pulled down. This to them is a severe punishment, for they generally have large families whom they dearly love. I have already seen numerous instances of this ; and, indeed, a number of houses belonging to those rebels who are at present in the army of the enemy will probably share the same fate within a short time. Among these Militia Captains are some very brave, intelligent and determined men, who are worthy of the greatest respect, and whom the Governors have no hesitation in inviting to sit at their tables. Tall pine-trees, with the bark peeled off and with a small flag fluttering at their tops, are placed before the houses of the Militia Captains and their Lieutenants, in order that their abodes may readily be found.

Nearly every Parish has a *seigneur* living in it. When the French first settled Canada, very large tracts or districts were given byt he Crown to members of the nobility, and to officers who had rendered great services. Such tracts were from three to four leagues long by the same in width, and the titled owners parcelled out portions of them to those who desired to build upon the land. In this way, Parishes and the houses in them originated. The *seigneur* therefore, virtually owns all the property in the Parish, or the land upon which the inhabitants have built; and every tenant must pay him a yearly sum—amounting to several piasters—as well as tithes consisting of calves, sheep, poultry, etc. * The *seigneur*, more-over, has the privilege of being the first buyer of all of his tenants' superfluous grain or cattle that they may wish to sell. His principal source of income, however, is derived from his mills; for the reason that all the farmers have to bring their grain to him to be ground; and this, in itself, brings in a very pretty rental. Again, if one of the inhabitants sells his house, the *seigneur* receives one sixth of the selling price. The so-called *châteaux* of the *seigneurs*, how-ever, are not to be compared with those that we have at home. A house similar to those I have already described, with one room more, and at the utmost having but two stories, is the home of the *seigneur*. Very often, indeed, the *seigneurie* is dwarfed into in-significance by the other houses in the Parish; for every now and then you will meet with very sub-stantial residences, built with taste and in the latest style of architecture. When Canada was ceded to England, a number of French *seigneurs* sold their *seig-neuries* to Englishmen, and then returned to France. The *seigneurs* have no courts in their Parishes, and as far as I am aware, no system of vassalage. The owners of *seigneuries* bear the names of ancient and distinguished French families, though they have lost much of their old-time splendor. All the inhabitants of the Parishes

---

* Thus, much of the land in New York State was sold under the same conditions, which eventually gave rise to the Anti-rent War.

are related to them ; and many of their children have become plain farmers themselves. The *seigneur* is not ashamed to marry a pretty girl belonging to one of his tenants; and thus his brothers-in-law may often be honest farmers or mechanics. Many of his tenants have bought their freeholds from him, and consequently no longer pay him ground-rent. It is for this reason that numbers of *seigneurs* may be seen who have fallen into a state of decadence, and who are hardly to be distinguished from the rest of their neighbors. Occasionally, however, some are met with who still live in brilliant style, and whom the Government seeks to draw into its service. There are numbers of them in the *suite* of General Carleton, acting as *aides-de-camps*. Notwithstanding their decadence, however, the poor *seigneurs* are treated with the same respect as of old ; and no inhabitant would dream of meeting his *seigneur* without showing him all proper deference. Several rich merchants of Quebec and Montreal, by the way, are the proprietors of their own *seigneuries.*

New houses are springing up yearly in all the Parishes. All *seigneurs* have still plenty of timber to sell. The ground belonging to a " habitation " is 4 *arpens* * in length and from 30 to 40 in depth. The new *habitant* has thus a large piece of ground which he can divide up with his children and grand-children

---

* A word of Gallic origin,—a furlong; being, according to Doomsday Book, equal to 100 perches.

whenever they wish to set up housekeeping for themselves. In preparing his land for cultivation, he first burns down the trees; and when they fall, he uses the timber thus obtained for his new house. He then lays bare the roots of the trees by digging; sets fire to them; and when they have been consumed, his land is ready for the plough. At first, he is content to live in a poor and miserable house—more like a hut than anything else—containing but one room and a kitchen. From time to time, as he increases his productive land by ridding it of the stumps, he adds additional rooms to his house; so that in the course of twenty years he has a good habitation and very excellent land. All the ground within a distance of one fourth of a league from the houses has now been cleared of timber, and consequently the *habitans* have fine fields. The forests of Canada have not been despoiled to any great extent. The trees which have been selected for removal have a fire built around their base, which generally burns until the trees fall. If this is not sufficient, a few blows of the axe finish the work. For this reason, the forests often present a desolate appearance; and as one looks upon the charred and withered trees, he easily imagines that they must have been struck by fire from heaven. These "clearings" in the forests yield very fine crops of grass and hay, thus furnishing most excellent fodder for the cattle. Nearly all Canadians—many of whom are young—build new habitations for themselves, and are presented by their parents with cattle and articles

100117

for housekeeping. " Be fruitful and multiply" seems to be their motto ; for the family of the new *habitant* soon begins to increase. He has, however, to work hard and live economically for a number of years before he is able to fill his barns with grain and enlarge his stock. Since the older sons receive help from their parents in establishing themselves in new homes, the younger sons generally inherit the old homestead.

In every house the *habitans* engage in various trades. In them you will find tavern-keepers, wine and liquor dealers, well-to-do merchants, shoemakers, tailors, wheelwrights, cabinet-makers, etc. In each Parish there is a post-house, having from five to six *calèches.* One English shilling, or seven *groschen*, is charged for every league gone over in a *calèche ;* and one is enabled by these vehicles to travel very rapidly. The ordinary post in Canada is as regular as with us at home. The *seigneurs*, the post-houses, and the houses of the Captains of Militia are exempted from furnishing quarters to the troops, as well as from providing conveyances in war-time.

Really, the Canadians are excellent people. Their ancestors are French, but they call themselves Canadians, and the English Government looks upon this with favor. They are austere rather than volatile or lively, and have lost much of the vivacity of their ancestors. They are the very reverse of *prévenant* and *engageant*, and it is difficult to gain their confidence ; but when you have gained it, they are with you heart and soul. By nature they have the true *droiture du*

0811303

cœur, and are inclined to fair dealing. Having once secured their trust, a scoundrel could easily persuade them to do unlawful things and bring about their ruin. For this reason many of them have taken sides with the rebels, without knowing why they did so. The principal instigators of these troubles have been Frenchmen and adventurers who drifted into Canada at the time of the war between England and France, and who have made them believe that France intends to send an army to Canada.

The Canadians are an intelligent people, and most of them are veritable *hommes d'esprit.* Their expressions and conversation are always to the point; and, in addressing strangers, or while talking with each other they are always polite without indulging in ridiculous compliments. They are talkative among themselves, but you seldom see them laughing, jumping about, dancing, or indulging in badinage. The worries of life, hard work, and trouble have caused their features to assume a severe look, which might lead you to believe that their faces were but masks hiding fierce and stealthy thoughts behind them. This impression disappears however, upon closer acquaintance. In view of the present times, many of them appear to be the possessors of guilty consciences, a fact that can be plainly read upon their countenances. I have indeed passed through Parishes in which the faces of all the *habitans* seemed to betray their rebellious tendencies. In such cases, the Canadian can be very malignant and treacherous. In one instance, Boilau, a

Captain of Militia in Chambly and an ardent royalist, was waylaid a. number of times by his nephew, who was a rebel, in order that he might scalp his uncle ! Again, Brigadier-General Gordon was treachously shot while in his *caléche* near his camp in the woods at Chambly.

No other nation can endure fatigue, labor, and hardship with greater fortitude. To suffer the pangs of hunger for several days without complaining is nothing new to them. Not a few of these people are at present serving in the army, although to do so they often have to drive from 100 to 200 leagues in their carts (*charettes*). *C'est pour le service du roi* is all that is required to be said in order to induce the Canadian cheerfully to undertake the work he has been ordered to do. They cannot endure rough treatment, such as knocks and blows; and no one will more bitterly complain of that kind of usage than they. This sensitiveness is no doubt caused by their finer feelings. They will tell you that a *pauvre Canadien* (poor Canadian) also has his feelings, and will make you the judge of their troubles and sufferings. To sum up, they wish to be treated in a courteous manner. Should you wish them to do anything for you, your request must be prefaced with kind words, otherwise they will either feel insulted or act treacherously. In fine, no other nation is more obliging than theirs if treated kindly. On the other hand, it will not do to be too kind and polite. In making your requests, you must combine a certain amount of firmness with your civility, that they may understand that you will submit to no remonstrance. None are better aware of this than the Captains of Militia, who find it necessary to maintain a more or less enforced obedience and to nip in the bud the first signs of disobedience.

In their housekeeping they are very orderly and exact ; nor can any other nation live so economically. During the summer the Canadian lives on bread as white as snow, milk, vegetables, and flour. He saves his cattle and poultry for the winter ; and then he is said to live in grand style ! Their thrift can be seen in their furniture and other household articles (dating from the time of Louis XIV.), all of which afford ample evidence of having passed down through many hands. Regarding money matters they are exceedingly close, and well they may be ; for you will seldom meet with a family having less than eight or ten children. Even when they have no need of money, you will not find them giving any of it away. Neither need you feel ashamed courteously to offer a lady with whom you may stand on a friendly footing, a few *sous* for the milk she may have given you with your coffee, for she will receive it as politely as you offer it. On the other hand, it will warm your heart to observe how hospitable they are among each other. A Canadian can go on a journey of a hundred miles, and without much trouble find quarters for himself and horse at whatever house he may chance to stop. He will enter, eat, drink, sleep, and gossip with his host

as unconcernedly as if he were at home ; and notwithstanding this you will meet with no "sponges." As
to beggars, they are unknown in Canada. The *habitans* regard each other as blood-relations ; and one
Parish will assume, if necessary, the burdens (i.e. taxes)
of another Parish, instead of trying to shift them upon
the other as with us at home. The Canadians are not
at all suspicious. Their barns are left unlocked ; their
cattle roam about the yard ; and most of their things
are not even put under lock and key. They will not
touch anything that does not belong to them. You
may safely give several guineas to the first Canadian
you chance to meet to have them changed, for he will
invariably return with the correct amount. Again, he
will gladly loan you his furniture, besides lending you
a helping hand whenever in his power, without
manifesting any signs that he would like to be paid
for the same. By paying him he will become the most
faithful and discreet of messengers, and can be sent
almost through the length and breadth of Canada.

The Canadians are also very cleanly. They love
tobacco, though I cannot understand how they can
smoke the strongest and most disgusting tobacco in
short pipes and to such excess. The ladies (every
woman in this country is styled *Madame*) love snuff ;
and no Canadian will reject a glass of rum. Still,
I have seen very few heavy drinkers or habitual
drunkards.

Fashion is under a ban in Canada. Nearly every
stitch the *habitant* wears upon his back is made by

himself. He makes his own *souliers des sauvages* [moccasins]; and he also manufactures a kind of shoe from dressed leather, made without heels and straps, and which, when new, does not look so very badly. In the winter we will have to try this shoe; for they tell us that our feet will freeze in our ordinary boots. Thickly knitted brown stockings are tied under the knee by a red woollen band. His breeches are either made of rough cloth, or from the hides of wild cattle tanned by himself. His shirts are tied in front, and made out of dotted home-spun goods similar to those worn by our peasants at home. His clothes are fastened about his hips by means of a thick woollen scarf, with tassels dangling at the ends. These scarfs are of all colors, according to the wearer's taste. A woollen hood (a Capuchin hood) is attached to the back of his coat, which he draws over his head in rough and wet weather. Hats are seldom worn; thick red colored bonnets, lined inside with white, being most generally affected by the Canadians. The Canadian dandy wears a jacket made of some kind of white frieze, ornamented in front by red-and-blue ribbons and several rosettes of the same material. This dress or jacket, which is fringed, is the national costume, and feels very comfortable and warm. Governor Carleton, when forced to travel among the Canadians in winter on government business, himself wears one of these jackets. In summer the *habitans* wear jackets of silesia, calico, or linen, with ribbons fluttering behind. Should one judge the Canadians by their clothes, he is liable to make serious mistakes; as he will often find a rich or prominent man wearing a miserable coat. People living in the cities, and well-to-do *habitans,* such as notaries, merchants, and the like, dress in the English or French fashion, but without wearing gold or silver jewelry. Artistic hair-dressing is unknown. The *habitant* ties his queue with a white ribbon. The ladies dress in the same style as their sex on the other side, and, whether rich or poor, put up their hair in a *chignon,* and also wear hoods fastened under the chin with colored silk ribbons. As yet, I have seen no lady with her hair curled. The rich wear in winter a cloth mantel (trimmed, perhaps, with fur), and in summer one made of light material, the capes attached to them being pulled over the head.

Every *habitant* has his horse, *calèche,* and sleigh. What he calls a *calèche* [calash] is the same as our carioles at home, with this difference: the wagon-box is capable of holding two persons, and the axle is longer. The driver sits in front upon a board seat, with both feet resting on the shafts. The entire *calèche* is made of pine, and I do not believe that you will find three *groschens'* worth of iron on it. The outer part of the wheels is without a tire, but the inner parts have iron casings. The axle to which they are attached is composed of plain wood, and the shafts are of thin wood. The body is also of wood, and is suspended from home-made leather straps or ropes. Some of the roads are so bad that one runs the risk of breaking his neck ; but it seldom happens that the *calèche* is broken, as the pine in this country is extraordinarily tough and hard. Canadian horses are well though lightly built, and, though of medium size, are strong. With a pair of large, round bells jingling about their necks, they can trot six leagues at a stretch over hills and mountains, through thick and thin. One of these horses can cover from twelve to fifteen leagues a day without eating; and, after un-hitching your horse at your journey's end, he is let loose in a paddock, where he eats his fill of grass. It is only in winter, and but seldom in summer, that horses are fed on oats. They are not shod in sum-mer but only in winter, when they are driven before a sleigh, which, by the way, is so light, as to almost go by itself. At any rate, you can make from two to two and a half German miles in such a vehicle in an hour. Caroches, chaises, etc., in fact all four-wheeled wagons, are unknown in Canada. Rich people have tops to their *calèches*, and sometimes have a team har-nessed to them. All carts have two wheels ; are also lightly built, and are used by the *habitant* to carry his grain and hay. The driver guides his horse by speak-ing to, and not by whipping, him—talking to him meanwhile, during the entire trip, as if he were a human being. The following are some of the expres-sions to be heard on the road : "*va doux, paresseux* [lazy beast], "*prenez, garde à vous, doucement,*" etc.*

---

* Mrs. General Riedesel gives an amusing account of her travels behind a *calèche* on her way to Three Rivers to join

The Canadians are expert boatmen. Every *habitant* is a hunter and a fisherman ; both of which vocations are within the reach of every one. There are but few ponds. An ox-horn is his powder-horn. Wild duck, snipe, and wild pigeons are plentiful ; while bears, rabbits, muskrats and beavers can be shot in the winter. However, as I am not as yet an expert in hunting, I will have to leave further details of this sport until some future time.

While the fine arts are unknown to the Canadians, it is not from lack of ability to learn. They know of nothing except what is going on within their own immediate circle. Regarding religion they are very devout, but ignorant. I have not found them intolerant in regard to their religious views ; at any rate, they do not as yet look upon me as a heretic. Their *curés* are mostly good and sociably disposed men with agreeable manners—some of them indeed, possessing considerable knowledge. Their churches do not contain

---

her husband. " The Canadians," she writes, "are everlastingly talking to their horses, and giving them all kinds of names. Thus, when they were not either lashing their horses or singing, they cried, ' *Allons, mon prince ! Pour mon général.*' Oftener, however, they said, '*Fi, donc, madame !*' I thought that this last was designed for me, and asked, ' *Plait-il ?*' ' Oh,' replied the driver, '*ce n'est que mon cheval, la petite coquine.*' (It is only the little jade, my horse.)" A very good picture of a *calèche*, with the driver seated on the fills, and driving merrily along, may be seen in " Weld's Travels in America, 1796–7."

many sacred paintings, a fact, perhaps, which may be accounted for on the score of expense. No convents are to be found in the country.* But few people are able to write, and the orthography of the rich who can write may be compared with that of our common classes at home. I have read letters written by Captain of Militia, Tournencour—a prominent banker and one of the wealthiest men in Canada—which would require a key in order to understand them. They write as they speak, and contract several words into one.

All Canadians, no matter how they may try to disguise it, still have a leaning towards French rule. The English Government is on guard however, and General Carleton's chief strength lies in the fact of his being able to ferret out all attempts in that direction without its being known from what sources he receives his information.

Canada exports yearly 1000 lasts [2000 tons] of wheat. She has, moreover, considerable trade in horses with other English colonies; and the many thousand head of cattle we have already devoured are but such a small proportion of those still remaining in Canada that we live in hopes of whetting our teeth on the flesh of many thousands more !

---

* All the convents had either been burned down or converted into barracks before this writer came to Canada. See letters farther on. Gen. Riedesel, however, speaks of a pleasant nunnery at Three Rivers, called the Convent of Ursulines.

FIRST CAMPAIGN OF THE BRUNS-WICKERS IN CANADA IN THE YEAR 1776.*

BATISCAMP, Nov. 3, 1776.

On the 24th of September, I left my ship to proceed to Quebec, where, on the following day, I had the opportunity of witnessing the burial of a Freemason. Two Masons, bearing standards draped in mourning, led the procession; these, in turn, were followed by the entire lodge marching in pairs according to their rank in that body; all being attired in full regalia, with fine white leather aprons extending down to their

---

* This is a complete daily journal having reference to the march of the Brunswickers from Sept. 24 to Nov. 3, 1776, by the author of " Private Letters from Canada," interspersed with numerous petty but characteristic details, and containing, particularly, an accurate topography of the entire region in Canada between Quebec and Lake Champlain. The latter feature will be the more welcome to our readers, since, as the author himself states in another part of his letters, complete land-charts of Canada are very scarce.—*Note by Schlözer.*

38

knees, and a mason's trowel at the side. The *frères terribles* walked to the grave with drawn swords. All the Masons were clothed in black ; and in place of mourning cloaks, they wore a fine white sash about two hands in width, extending from the right shoulder down to the left side, in the same manner in which the Hanoverians wear their scarfs. In place of crape, they had a folded white cloth, a yard and a half long, hanging down from the right side of their hats. Following the body came two English preachers attired also in mourning habits, they, in turn, being followed by a detachment of one officer, four under-officers, and three hundred men of the English militia of Quebec. These last carried arms—the deceased having been a militia officer. Upon the coffin, which was borne by the lay-brothers, were placed the dead man's sword and his masonic regalia. Immediately after the coffin came, in ordinary civilian's dress, the militia company to which the deceased had belonged. A more impressive silence and a more quiet funeral I have never witnessed.

To-day the battalion of Bärmer disembarked at Quebec, and immediately began their march to join the main army.

On the 26th, half of Specht's regiment also disembarked and followed them. We marched through the city of Quebec, passing out through the gate. Here we saw, lying in mournful ruins, the suburb St. John, which had been burned the previous year by the rebels in their attack upon the town. We passed some very handsome country-seats belonging to wealthy citizens of that city, several of which had been laid in ashes by the rebels through hatred of their owners. We had a good road, and rested our weary bones in the Parish of St. Foye, two and a half leagues from Quebec—a league is nearly an hour and a half's walk or five eighths of a German mile. Who would not be tired in making even a short march, after being confined for thirteen weeks on shipboard? This parish lies on the northern bank of the St. Lawrence River, and contains very good houses, built of stone and surrounded by excellent fields, meadows, commons and gardens.

On the 27th, Rhetz's regiment disembarked and started on a similar march. Meanwhile, we proceeded on ours, and, soon after leaving St. Foye, encountered such villainous defiles between rocky hills that when we first caught sight of them our thoughts at once reverted to the Hartz Mountains.* An unusually steep road led us up and down hills between masses of rock, which, however, were only of moderate height. The river, which, at Cape Rouge, empties into the St. Lawrence, was crossed by us on a ferry. Again, we were obliged to pass over a steep and rocky road leading through woods and underbrush until we once

---

* From the outskirts of Brunswick, on a clear day, the Hartz Mountains can easily be seen. In my walks in the vicinity of that town I have often looked upon them. No wonder then that the thoughts of this Brunswick officer reverted to that familiar landscape near his home!

more came within a short distance of the St. Lawrence, which, of course, lay on our left. On the right, a mountain covered with boulders and an impenetrable forest towered aloft like a wall, having at its base a large number of immense pebble stones [boulders] which had rolled far into the river. Some of these stones were from 6 to 8 yards in diameter. Whether they had rolled down from the mountain, set free by the rains of many years, or were originally in the river-bed, I cannot say. At length, we arrived at the parish of St. Augustin. While the houses are scattered among the mountains, the beautiful fields and meadows which belong to them extend along the river-bank. This parish is a large one ; and here we saw, for the first time, genuine wooden buildings. We continued our march until we reached the parish of *Pointe aux Trembles*, where we took up our quarters, having covered a distance of 7 leagues. This parish is more than one and a half German leagues in length, and, as a general thing, has good stone houses situated at distances of from three to four hundred paces apart.*
To-day we received gratifying news of the safe arrival of the ship " Wiesland " at *Isle le Bic* in the St. Lawrence, having on board nearly three companies of Specht's regiment.

28th : We resumed our march along the banks of the St. Lawrence, and passed through the parish

---

* A " pace," when used by a military man, means about two and one half feet.

Larreaux, its church being built close to the river. In order to cross the Jaques Cartier River—a name derived from the first settler* in the neighborhood— we were obliged to seat ourselves in large boats, having first unpacked our baggage.   On the other side of the river we found other conveyances.   We had, however, to climb several steep and rocky elevations ; and having accomplished this feat, we took up our quarters in the beautiful parish of *Cap Santé*, four leagues in length, and the dwellings of which lie 800 paces apart. The church here is the newest and handsomest in all Canada, and its style of architacture is unequalled. Its three small doors are covered with white lead.   The house of the curé is modern as well as large.

29th: We continued our march, and on reaching the extremity of this Parish (*Cap Santé*) we met with two large English guard-ships at anchor in the St. Lawrence.   Notwithstanding a wretchedly cold rain, we found the roads to be level and in good condition.   After covering three leagues we took up our quarters in the Parish of *Chambeant* on the St. Lawrence—the Parish *l'Aubiegniére* being in view on the opposite bank.

On the 30th, we took a day of rest, that we might get in a stock of flour so as to be able to bake.

Oct. 1st, we crossed the small river Maquiere, or, rather, our conveyances forded it, which was easily done at ebb tide.   The soldiers, however, had to be

---

* The discoverer of the Saint Lawrence, 1534.

ferried over. We continued our march through the Parish of *les Grondines,* which lies at quite a distance from the St. Lawrence, and where the breeding of cattle is far ahead of an otherwise not remarkable agricultural people. After proceeding five leagues, we rested in the very large and beautiful Parish of St. Anne, which has an extremely well built and rich *seigneurie.* Here we saw large quantities of hazel-hens, wild ducks, partridges and rabbits. In this Parish, I met several German *habitans,** who had formerly come into this Province with the French armies.

On the 2d, we crossed the river St. Anne in bateaux near the church, at which point we were strongly reminded of the Weser. On the opposite side, we were met by *caleches* and carts—the Parish of St. Anne extending also on this bank of the river. We marched through numerous woods and underbrush; and in the latter, we continually came upon flocks of one hundred and more black thrushes. In this underbrush, also, we met with many cotton-shrubs bearing ripe fruit.† These peculiar shrubs invariably grow

---

* A name applied to the inhabitants of Lower Canada who are of French descent.

† "The plant here referred to is the Cat-tail or Cotton-rush, *Typha latifolia.* The heads of ripe seed do grow, as described, singly; and the down is still largely used by the inhabitants of Lower Canada for stuffing beds and pillows." —*Letter from Prof. James Fletcher, Botanist of the Experimental Farm, Ottawa, Canada. Jan.* 9, 1891. Some of the New Jersey farmers also use Cat-tails for the same purpose.

singly ; and the *habitans* stuff their beds with its cotton, for which purpose it cannot be equalled. Finally we arrived at the Parish *Batiscan*, where I now live.

This parish is none of the best ; and though it extends, laterally, to a distance of five leagues, the houses lying within it are, as a general rule, most wretched. On the opposite side of the river is the Parish of St. *Ricom*. The St. Lawrence, which is a good 200 paces from my quarters, is here fully one half a German mile wide ; and so deep that three-masted ships can easily float upon it. The river Batiscan flows through the middle of the Parish, and you can easily cross it on thick planks, or, if you prefer, with canoes. It is a trifle wider than the St. Anne River. This very day we drove through the Parish *Champlin*, where Mr. Blanc, a Captain *de Milice* [militia] and a native of Geneva, became my good friend. We had marched only four leagues, having been greatly hindered by rivers. The largest of our English war-frigates, "The Bride," lay at anchor at *Champlin*. She carries thirty-six guns. The Parish of *Chantilly* lies on the opposite side of the river.

On the 3d, we marched through the Parish of St. *Madelone* [Magdalene], which is opposite the Parish of *Rosencour*. We were forced to cross numerous creeks ; and, as a consequence, also many bridges. A Canadian bridge is a queer thing. It consists entirely of a number of beams or round tree-trunks placed side by side. Should one of these beams or trunks break, it does not matter, as the others retain their positions.

These bridges, however, must be dangerous to cross at night, especially for horses ; in fact, some of our horses broke their legs as it was. We passed a large wood composed chiefly of pine, fir, ash, birch, alder, wild apple and oak trees which grew amid tangled underbrush and countless wild shrubs. Here, we also fell in with the wigwams of numerous Indians, who, however, were hogs compared with other savages whom we had met—they lived in such a beastly manner. Pursuing our journey five and a half leagues further, we came to the river St. Francis, also known as Three Rivers or *Trois Rivière*, from the fact that the river St. Maurice here divides and enters the St. Lawrence by three channels. This river is wider than the Saale. Again, we gentlemen had to step into shallops and allow ourselves to be ferried over. An Indian, for two shillings, did me the honor of carrying me across the river like the wind in his birch-bark canoe. After crossing, we still had to march a good league before arriving at the town of Three Rivers, where we dried our clothes, it having rained the entire day.

Three Rivers, although the oldest French colonial town in Canada, is small and straggling. It contains scarcely three hundred houses, most of which are of wood and but one story high. Still, many merchants occupy them as residences. M. de Tonneucourt [Tonnancour], the Colonel of Militia in this place, is one of the wealthiest persons in all Canada. He is a large contractor, merchant, corn- and cattle-dealer, and a Jew. Nothing in the way of trade comes amiss to him. He will sell you half an ounce of pepper, or retail you a glass of brandy in his house ; while, at the same time, he supplies the larger part of Canada with wine at wholesale. Sometimes he lives on a magnificent, and at others on a small, scale ; has numerous outlying country-houses ; likes to loan money on houses and farms ; and, in short, is universally known as the " Pope of Canada." The Convent of the Recollets has been abolished ; the former Government-House turned into a barrack for 300 men ; and the Ursuline Convent converted into a hospital for our troops. The chief resident Curé bears the title of Grand Vicar. Many pretty and lively girls are met with in this town who dress themselves very neatly. Quite a number of *Seigneurs* have here their winter residences. A 20-gun frigate lay anchored on the St. Lawrence, which flows close by the city. An extremely important magazine is also located here ; and occasionally you will meet with exceedingly nice houses furnished very respectably.

On the 4th, we marched over very dirty, muddy and swampy roads filled with pitfalls, passing through the Parish of *Pointe au Lac*,* a wretchedly poor place. At this point, the St. Lawrence widens out into a large lake, called *Lac de St. Pierre*, which is three

---

* *Pointe du Lac :* also called Tonnancour—probably named after the merchant of the same name, mentioned a Page or two back.

leagues in width. We passed the little Muschiche River,* and after making six leagues, remained over night in the Parish of *Machitiche.* Upon the other side of *Lac St. Pìerre* lies the Parish of *St. Antoine* or *Lefevre* on a bay of the same name, between which and the lake stretches a long neck of land called *Longue Pointe.*

On the 5th, we passed, on our march, the large Parish *au Loup* and the river of the same name. We crossed also, the Maskinonge River in boats, marched six leagues further, and slept that night in the Parish of *Maskinonge,*† which meets with my approval.

The 6th was a day of rest.

On the 7th, we had a passable road, through a long straggling wood about three leagues in length; though frequently we were up to our knees in mud and water. We crossed the river *Chicot,* as well as the little river *Basté,* on a float [raft ?]. We had now marched four and a half leagues, and accordingly rested for the night in the excellent Parish of *Barties.* The *seigneur* living here—an Englishman named Colbert—has a fine castle fitted up in the best of taste. He has laid out a new Parish three leagues in length, extending laterally from *Barlier,* and named it York. On my return, I passed through it, and have seen

---

* The Mascouche River in Lower Canada, which falls into the river St. John about twelve miles before the latter joins the St. Lawrence.

† So named after the fish Mascalinga, or Muscalonge—as Pike Co., in Pennsylvania, is called after that fish.

a new Parish in its infancy ; and anything more wretched and forlorn cannot be imagined. At *Barlier, Lac St. Piérre* forms various islands, the one nearest *Barlier* and uninhabited being called *Isle au Custus.* It is four leagues in length by nearly the same in width. In the rear of this lies the far larger and inhabited *Isle du Pas.*

On Oct. 8th, twenty-two bateaux were sent to us from Sorel to convey Specht's regiment and baggage across [up] the St. Lawrence to that village. They were all royal bateaux, of which the army has over one thousand. Such a bateau, or large boat, can carry from seven to eight thousand pounds in weight and twenty-eight or thirty people. Our soldiers, who have learned the art perfectly since they have been in Canada, were obliged to row—English soldiers, thoroughly understanding navigation, holding the steering-oars. We rowed three and a half leagues before arriving at Sorel, which is situated on the south bank of the St. Lawrence. At this place, the large and important Sorel—or, as it is really called, the river Richelieu*— flows into it from Lake Champlain in two branches, one on each side of the village. We landed at Sorel, where we found an English detachment of one hundred and thirty men, and also a very large magazine ftom which we replenished our stock. At the mouth of the Sorel were about forty two- and three-masted English transport-ships whose crews had recently

---

* Now the St. John's River.

formed part of our army at Lake Champlain. An English frigate was also on guard here. As the rough weather and the passage across [up] the river had greatly detained us, and as, moreover, the roads beyond Sorel, which led through thick woods, were execrable, we were obliged, after 8 o'clock in the morning, to leave several companies behind us. The rest of the troops, however, managed to reach the Parish of St. Thomas, where we again met with two English frigates on guard in the Sorel River. Many of the inhabitants of these Parishes are in the service of the rebels : among them, a *habitant*, named Nugent, who, only eight years ago, was a hair-dresser in Montreal, but is now the high and mighty colonel of a regiment of Bostonians ! The distance between Sorel and St. Thomas is three leagues.

On the 9th we crossed numerous creeks over which dangerous log-bridges, similar to those I have previously described, were placed. These bridges were thrown across the streams so low that one was obliged first to go down a steep descent about the height of two houses, and then ascend the embankment on the opposite side. At nearly every 200 paces we would encounter such a bridge. This condition of things was caused by the water having carried away the earth on each side. We covered to-day but three leagues— in fact, we advanced only as far as the large and beautiful Parish of *St. Denis.* Here were stationed, for the protection of the transports, a Hesse-Hanau and Brunswick detachment of 84 men. On the other side of the Sorel was the Parish of *St. Antoine.* The inhabitants of this Parish looked as if they were rebelliously inclined.

On the 10th we passed through the Parish of St. Charles. At this place we crossed the Sorel in a ferryboat that seemed frail enough to drown us, and took up our quarters in the Parish of *Bel Veulle* [*Belœil?*], which is over 3 leagues in length. Five leagues further, and opposite, is the Parish of *St. Louis.* Von Bärner's battalion were to-day quartered in the Parish of *St. Thérèse.*

On the 11th, while on our march, we saw the *Isle au Cerf* in the Sorel. To-day, we only advanced as far as the Parish of Chambly, 1⅓ leagues distant, where were stationed, for the protection of an important magazine and a train containing a large quantity of ammunition, an English colonel with a detachment. Upon the river were anchored two English sloops-of-war carrying eight to ten guns.

Fort Chambly, lying on the Sorel, has had its interior burned out by the rebels. The fort is square and built entirely of masonry. It is now undergoing repairs ; and barracks, for from two to three hundred men, are constructing inside of the walls. Beyond Chambly we cannot go with bateaux on account of rapids which extend from this place to a distance of three leagues. The river here is wide but not deep ; and on its bottom can be seen innumerable large stones over which the water dashes itself into foam. The bateaux and small vessels are therefore unloaded at this point, and their cargoes, consisting of all the army supplies, carried in *charettes* [carts] a distance of three leagues before they can be reloaded into the boats. All the vessels that were used by our army on Lake Champlain were trans-ported on land piece by piece from *Chambly* to a dis-tance of 3 leagues, when they were again put together. Major-General Riedesel was stationed, with two regi-ments, upon *Isle aux Noix.* This island lies in the Sorel near where that river opens into Lake Champlain. At *Chambly* the Parishes cease.

On our arrival at *Chambly* we found that the main army [under Carleton] had already embarked and started for lake Champlain, partly in ships and partly in bateaux. First of all, however, I must describe that Lake, although, as yet, I have not seen it myself. Above *Chambly* and on the Sorel lies Fort St. John. Here Bärner's battalion was to-day encamped, except-ing the Jägers [Rifle-men], who had gone forward with the main army. Above* St. John, and the again navigable Sorel, lies the *Isle aux Noix.* On this island, which is uninhabited, General Riedesel lay encamped. A little way further, and you reach the large Cham-plain Sea, across the middle of which runs the bound-

---

* This word " above" proves, among other things, that the writer was a careful observer, and had taken pains to acquaint himself accurately with the topography of the country. *Hadden* (who, if he had been writing, would have written *below*) and most all writers at this time invariably speak as if the St. John River, and Lake Champlain ran *south*, like the Hudson.

ary line between Canada and New York. Then, again, upon the right, or western bank of the lake, is a well-known cape, called, *Pointe aux Terres*, where General Carleton lay encamped with the *corps d'armée.* Moreover, in the lake itself are to be found the *Isle aux deux Tetes, Pointe aux Pommes, Isle la Motte,* and *Isle la Grande*, etc. During the day the regiments were obliged to row ; and towards night they landed, and, building fires in the woods, cooked their evening meal. Our naval force upon the lake consists of the ship " Carleton,"12 guns ; " Lady Marie," 14 guns ; " L'Inflexible," 30 guns ; and the " Radeau," * carrying 6 guns, and also having upon deck 8 or 10 small cannon. The "Armide," and " Baleine," were 24-gun ships having 12-pounders at the fore, and, when brought end to end, served as a battery.

On the 12th, Specht's regiment had a day of rest, and united once more with that of Rhetz's.

On the 13th, both regiments occupied a camp in common at Chambly, but kept themselves in constant readiness to march to the advanced portion of the army. However, on the 15th, we heard that General Carleton had surprised, attacked, and defeated the

---

* " The Radeau was an unique structure which is often mentioned in the naval annals of the northern lakes. It was scarcely more than a raft or floating battery, but constructed with great solidity and strength. It was protected only by low and slight bulwarks, but, armed with the heaviest ordnance, it was a powerful and effective craft."—*General Horatio Rogers, in " Hadden's Journal."*

enemy's fleet between *Isle au Chapon* and the main-land, and had driven the remainder of the fleet into Cumberland Bay.

On the 17th, we further learned that the enemy's fleet was entirely ruined, it having been burnt, and, in part, sunk by boring holes in the vessels. Most of the rebels saved themselves, however, by taking to their bateaux. We have bored holes into or burned the following vessels, viz.: the " Royal Savage," carry-ing eight 6-pounders and four 4-pounders, and which was commanded by the notorious General Arnold *— a former horse-dealer, but who saved himself after first, with his own hands, setting fire to his vessel; the " Revenge," carrying two 4-pounders and six 3-pound-ers; the " Enterprise," with ten 4-pounders; " Le Cutter," with one 12-pounder and four 6-pounders; the " Tremble," with one 18-pounder, one 12-pounder, and six 6-pounders; the " Washington," carrying one 14-pounder, one 12-pounder, two 9-pounders, and six 6-pounders; the " Congress," of the same armament as the " Washington;" the " Philadelphia," with one 12-pounder, two 9-pounders; the " New York," car-rying the same number of guns as the " Philadelphia;" and the " Jersey," " Providence," " New Haven,"

---

* The Germans seem to have had a poor opinion of Arnold—one of the bravest and best generals the Conti-nental army ever had, and to whom is really due the entire credit of the victory of both battles of Saratoga. Thus, in a " List of American Generals for 1778 " in *Schlözer*, Arnold is described as an " apothecary, a bankrupt, and a swindler."

" Spitfire," and " Boston," also of the same complement of guns. Two vessels, that were sent to Ticonderoga, got off in safety. Thereupon General Carleton advanced as far as Crown Point, just as the rebels had evacuated it, after having first set it on fire. We learn, however, that the flames were extinguished by our army before they had gained much headway. Meanwhile, the rebels have withdrawn to a fortified camp at Fort Carillon [Ticonderoga], which very likely will become the seat of war next spring. None of our corps were engaged in the naval battle.

On October 20th and 21st, the army began their march into winter quarters. We hold the key to Canada, because we are now masters of Lake Champlain. Three thousand men are to remain at Crown Point, under the command of Brigadier Fraser. This force is made up of Indians, Canadians, grenadiers, and the riflemen (Jägers) of the Eleventh Regiment. Upon *Pointe aux Fer* and the *Isle aux Noix* Bärner's battalion is to be stationed. Our grenadiers will be placed in the Parish *St. Antoine* and *St. Denis ;* the Hesse-Hanaus in *Barties* and *Masquinonge*. The regiment of Prince Frederick will leave Quebec and go to *Marchishe [Machise]* and *Point au Loup*. Both of these regiments—that is, those of Hesse-Hanau and Prince Frederick—are under the command of Brigadier-General Gall. The dragoons and Von Riedesel's regiment will go into winter quarters at Three Rivers, *Pointe au Lac* and *Cap de Madelane*. Specht's regiment goes to *Cham-*

bly and *Batiscamp*, and Rhetz's to St. Anne and *Les Grondines*, both being under the command of Brigadier-General Specht. Two English regiments are to proceed to Quebec, which is to be the headquarters of General Carleton. General von Riedesel will take up his quarters at Three Rivers. Regarding the disposition of the English regiments, I do not, as yet, know; but this is certain, that the question of winter quarters for all has not yet been fully decided and is still under consideration. This much, however, I do know, viz. : that the parishes on the other side of the St. Lawrence are to be garrisoned. At present, from six to twelve men are quartered in a house, which is too much in Canada.

We are returning from *Chambly* to *Batiscamp* by the same route that we came.

Our army now consists of twelve English regiments, the names of which, excepting those of General Carleton and my Lord Cavendish, I am unable to name. I know, however, that a part of the army is made up of one regiment of dragoons, one battalion of grenadiers, and four regiments of Brunswickers. In addition to these, there are nearly 2000 Canadians serving as volunteers, besides 800 to 1000 Indians under the command of Captain Carleton (a nephew of General Carleton), who paints his face, wears a ring in his nose, and dresses like a savage. His wife is a "My Lady" and a sister to the wife of General Carleton. Both ladies have but recently arrived from

Europe. Lady von Riedesel, however, has not yet come.

About four days since, we heard for the first time of General Howe's fortunate battle on the 27th of August last. And would it be believed ! We received this piece of news by way of Quebec ; for by way of the South you can hear nothing of what is going on in the other Colonies. A communication with Carillon once opened up, it will be easy to correspond, by way of Albany, with New York, New England and Virginia. The battle occurred on Long Island. The English and Hessians stormed the enemy's entrenchments, scaled and carried them. Those captured are 3 generals (among them Lord Stirling), 4 colonels, 18 captains, 42 lieutenants, 11 ensigns, 1 aide major, 30 sergeants, and 1800 soldiers. Between 3000 and 4000 rebels are killed or wounded. On our side, we lost in killed and wounded 1 colonel, 3 captains, 12 officers, and not much over 500 men. The enemy left behind them their camp and artillery. General Howe immediately occupied the city of New York, and indeed rescued it from destruction ; for the rebels intended to set it on fire, and would have done so, had they not had a hospital containing several thousand men, whom it was impossible to remove readily. More accurate details are awaited with anxiety. Lieutenant-General Burgoyne will shortly sail for England to pass the winter. My correspondence will now be closed for at least four months, because the St. Lawrence begins to freeze up at the end of November, and consequently no letters can leave Quebec. Regarding our officers: we have lost by death, Lieutenant Katte and Ensign Unverzagt; this is all. The health of our regiments is good. That of Specht's up to date has lost 1 drummer and 8 men—all of whom were Brunswickers. It will astonish me, if the winter in Canada is as severe as they say it is.

PRIVATE LETTER FROM CANADA, WHICH ARRIVED IN LOWER SAXONY AUG. 1st, 1777.

PARISH OF ST. ANNE, MARCH 9—APRIL 20, 1777.*

Your letter, dated Sept. 3, arrived on Dec 13th, 1776, and was received by me with great pleasure. Up to the present time, but few have had the good luck to receive letters from the Old World, and, doubtless, many are even now lying in various places. It is known to a certainty that the English Lieutenant-Colonel MacLean, who is also Adjutant-General of the army, has in his possession a large number of letters brought with him from England; but where he and his vessel is, is still a matter of conjecture. It may be that, not daring to venture up the St. Lawrence River, he has put into Halifax for the winter; and should such be the case, we may soon expect to receive letters from home. For the European news you have given me I am deeply indebted to you. The

---

* This letter, apparently, was written to the writer's mother and brother conjointly.

different items are veritable tidbits, which we may look for in vain, especially in the winter-time, in the Quebec newspapers, though, in other respects, they contain quite valuable pieces of Canadian news.

You had the kindness to manifest great interest at our supposed lack of the necessaries of life. For the consolation of our friends at home, however, I am forced to state that the account given thereof was not true ; neither was it intended for a true statement of affairs. Up to the present, we have had abundance of very good beef, pork and mutton ; and since the 20th of February there has been no want of chickens, capons, geese, ducks, partridges and rabbits. There was, also, no lack of white cabbages, turnips, beets and excellent peas and beans, though it is true that we could get no cauliflower, lentils and other varieties of turnips. We also had to forego the pleasure of eating the venison of the deer, roe and wild-boar ; but your cook will tell you that many varieties of dishes may be made with the different articles I have already enumerated. Furthermore, let me assure you that every now and then we have excellent fish ; and that fine pastry can be made with flour and good butter. Roasted young bear-meat, beaver-tails, and caribou also taste well ; and when placed upon the table not only give it an epicurean appearance, but would be apt to convince you that the eye and palate can be appeased in Canada, as well as elsewhere. My beloved countrymen of Lower Saxony, however, can always flatter themselves that they alone possess the art of smoking, pickling and curing meats as well as making bolognas; nor will the natives of Suabia, Upper Saxony, the Rhine Provinces and the Canadians ever be able to equal them! Neither must you imagine that our common soldiers in this place are deprived of anything in favor of their officers. Both the former and the latter must take their provisions as they get them, for which they are charged daily one and a half pence. To the credit of our General-in-Chief Carleton be it said that through his efforts the German soldier receives daily, for this sum, $1\frac{1}{2}$ lbs. of beef and $1\frac{1}{2}$ lbs. of flour—an allowance which even the most fastidious stomach can endure. In addition to the above allowance, the soldier also receives excellent English peas and very good Irish butter.

Canadians unite in declaring that they have never experienced such a winter as the one we have just passed through. As for ourselves, we have noticed no perceptible difference between the cold here and that of our own country, though we were astonished at the even temperature. Since the 24th of last November, when we had our first snow and ice, we have had neither rain nor thaw; in consequence of which the snow and ice have been with us ever since. There have been numerous and heavy falls of fine, dry snow, which seldom last longer than twelve hours. It can, therefore, easily be imagined that the earth becomes covered with ice and snow to a depth of five or six feet. The natural weight of the snow, and the sun, which is warmer in Canada than with us at home, contract the snow into a solid mass upon which you can walk, and ride, if necessary, on cold days. The deep snow, the immense and dense forests, the thinly-settled distrıcts and level fields, the numerous large rivers and lakes, and the cold, penetrating north and northwest winds cause Canada to be colder than its natural situation would warrant. For persons with weak lungs these winds are dangerous; and when they are raging it becomes impossible to keep the room warm.

The entire army wears during the winter a peculiar costume, consisting of overalls made of cloth, and extending from the feet up to the waist, a pair of large mittens, and a cloth cap covering the head, neck, and shoulders. The English regiments wear, in addition, *capots Canadiens.* The St. Lawrence River, which, as a rule, becomes solidly frozen every winter, has not, up to the month of February, formed an ice-bridge. Prior to the 16th of that month, no ice-bridge had formed between Three Rivers and Quebec. Above the former town the current destroyed one of these bridges, and the detached cakes of ice, having become jammed at our parish of St. Anne, and also at that of *Les Grondines,* gave us two ice-bridges on the 17th, which, however, only lasted until the 19th. One experiences a curious sensation in driving for the first time across a river, say three fourths of a German mile wide, upon one of these bridges, and seeing the open and raging water at hardly two paces from you on either side. You imagine that the ice is giving way beneath you. It cracks, and at times you jump over crevices a hand in width. The Canadians venture in their *carioles* upon ice only four inches in thickness.

Now, dear Mamma, I will tell you something about Canadian domestic economy. In the middle of September the Canadians have a kind of Slaughtering Carnival, in comparison with which all similar events in Europe sink into insignificance. Within a period of from eight to ten days, all the fat four-footed animals and all the plump fowl in Canada are sacrificed. The cattle are cut up into pieces suitable for roasting or boiling, according to the taste of the owner, and the poultry are plucked of their feathers without dipping them into hot water as with us at home. The meat of both is then handed over to the care of Dame Nature until it is thoroughly frozen, when it is placed in *hangards* [sheds], so constructed that the wind sweeps through them from all sides; and whenever a piece of meat is wanted from time to time, it is taken out of these receptacles.

And now, dear Brother, for a few words in reply to your letter which now lies before me, and which, by the way, consists of but one and one-sixteenth of a page of writing-paper ! It seems to me that you still possess the qualities of a German Pliny, although I could wish that as long, at least, as I remain in America you would regard me with more consideration and manifest more of the characteristics of a Cicero ! Understand, Brother, once for all, that I am not quite yet, as you would insinuate, a Canadian pack-horse !

The best of my kit, it is true, I carry with me in my pocket, but my baggage proper goes by *Caleches, Charettes, Carioles, Truines, Bateaux, Canots* [canoes], or barques. However, let us now talk a little about hunting.

No game, dear Brother, worth speaking of is to be found in the neighborhood of the Parishes, the *habitans* having exterminated all the wild animals in the vicinity of their farm-houses. In fact, to enjoy real hunting, it is essential that you join one of the numerous Indian nations. You must accustom yourself to their manner of living, eating, sleeping, marching, and swimming, and also be able to travel four or five hundred leagues into the wilderness. The hunting trips that these savages undertake over mountains, rivers, lakes and morasses, and the means they employ to surmount all difficulties are beyond belief. They will go fifty or sixty German miles into a forest, build cabins there, and, leaving some of their companions behind, diverge in all directions in parties of two and three, and shoot anything they may encounter. At the end of four or five weeks, they will return to their general camp, which they can find as easily as if a plain and direct road led to it. Generally speaking, an Indian is able to travel many hundred leagues through wildernesses, overcoming all obstacles in his way, and without deviating from a straight course. Trees, leaves, rivers and other natural objects serve him the same purpose as a compass. This is a fine instinct, born with him and not acquired by use, experi-

ence or long study ; and when it begins to dawn upon
your mind that these savages can tell (as is very often
the case) to what nation a man belongs by examining
his footsteps ; when you learn furthermore, that he
can follow a trail through bushes and briers in the dark,
simply guided by his sense of smell, the same as our
hunting- and bird-dogs, you are apt to be astonished at
the qualities that God seems to have endowed these
people with, and which you were wont to believe
could only be possessed by animals. You will often
find Canadians and Englishmen hunting with these
people, or, more properly speaking, living in a wild
state among them for a number of years. Indeed, not
a year passes that a number of adventurers do not
join these Indian tribes ; influenced, it may be, either
by a wish to acquire a knowledge of the country, or
by a love of hunting, or by a desire to accumulate a
stock of furs, and establish with them at the same
time a system of trade and barter. Captain Carleton
of the 31st English Regiment and first aide-de-camp
to his uncle, the Governor and General, has lived with
the Indians a number of years in this manner. He
went through all the severe ordeals they subject themselves to in order to show their fortitude, and had
himself tattooed with the signs and totems with which
they are accustomed to decorate themselves. He even
went so far as to take a wife from among them, and
he asserts that the hours he spent with them were
the happiest of his life. You cannot imagine a more
refined, gentle, friendly, well-mannered, and, at the

same time, a more unaffected man than Captain Car-leton; and although his constitution has become wrecked and delicate, he still continues to command the Indians who constitute our advanced guard, and by whom he is greatly beloved.* His present wife is a very handsome woman, a "my lady" and the sister of the wife of General Carleton.

But, you ask, have we had plenty of amusement this winter ? I answer, right good ! You see, there are a number of *seigneurs* and *curés* in our neighbor-hood, and with their help and that of our officers in

---

* Captain Christopher Carleton (the officer here alluded to), a nephew of General Guy Carleton, is often confused with Major Thomas Carleton, a younger brother of that general. Christopher (now Major), when the British in-vaded the northern frontier of New York in 1780, had com-mand of the force which crossed Lake Champlain, and which consisted of 1000 men, regulars, loyalists and Indians. He was a brave and zealous officer, for which qualities he was complimented by General Haldimand. He became a lieu-tenant-colonel in the army, Feb. 19, 1783; and died at Quebec June 14, 1787. " For the last eleven years of his life he served in Canada, with an occasional visit to England only ; and he returned to Quebec for the last time, from one of these visits, Oct. 18, 1786, in the ship " Carleton," accompanied by his wife, Lady Anne Carleton, who was the second daughter of the second Earl of Effingham and an elder sister of the wife of Sir Guy Carleton, and who, after the death of her husband, returned to England." For a more detailed account of Major Christopher Carleton, see General Horatio Rogers in *Hadden's Journal.*

the vicinity we have been enabled to have a convivial, sociable, happy, and at times a "high old time"! *

Our *seigneur* at St. Anne, a passably rich man, a *Grand Inspecteur des Forêts et des Eaux royales* and an *aide-de-camp* of General Carleton, paid us a number of visits accompanied by friends, among whom were ladies from the city. Besides which, he has given us quite a number of little *fêtes* at his country-seat. The *curés*, also, are not to be despised. They are good royalists, and, being the possessors of good livings, are able to furnish dinners for twenty persons and provide the same with good wines. The *curé* at Batiscan, M. le Fevre, has given several very elegant *fêtes* in honor of General von Riedesel, and has not forgotten his neighbors at St. Anne.

On Dec. 28th, [1776,] Brigadier-General Specht and myself started to drive from St. Anne to Quebec, both to pay our respects to General Carleton and, at the same time, to attend a *fête* to which we had been formally invited. We passed the night with Lieutenant-Colonel Ehrenkrook at *Cap Santé;* and on the 30th paid our respects to his Excellency, and dined with him. In the evening we supped with Lieutenant-Governor Cramahé. On the 31st there was a great festival; that day being celebrated as the first anniversary of the deliverance of Quebec, on which occasion the rebels lost their great leader, General Montgomery. At 9 o'clock in the

---

* This is the exact expression in the text.

morning, a thanksgiving service was held in the Cathedral, at which *Monseigneur*, the Bishop, officiated. Eight unfortunate Canadians who had sided with the rebels were present, with ropes about their necks, and were forced to do penance before all in the church, and crave pardon of their God, Church and King. At 10 o'clock, the civic and military authorities, as well as all visiting and resident gentlemen, whether Canadian or English, assembled at the Government-House. All the resident gentlemen of Quebec, in accordance with their rank as officers of the militia, wore green suits with *paille* [straw] facings, waistcoats, knee-breeches, and silver epaulettes upon their shoulders. At 10.30, his Excellency came out of his room, and received congratulations. At 11, accompanied by Major-General Riedesel, Brigadier Specht and all of the officers and English gentlemen present, he left for a large square in front of the Recollets' Convent,* where the French militia, or Canadian citizen-soldiery of Quebec, were drawn up in eight companies. They fired off three trains of gunpowder, lit bonfires, and shouted *Vive le Roi!* From here the company proceeded to the " Upper Town" where we attended religious services in the English church. Here the roar of cannon from the citadel intermingled with the *Te Deum*, while enthusiastic citizens shot off shot-guns and muskets from their windows. At 3 o'clock, the General gave a dinner to sixty persons,

---

* For a sketch of the Recollets' Convent, see Appendix.

at which no ladies, except the two Lady Carletons, were present.

In the evening, at six, the entire company started for the large English *auberge* [hotel], where over ninety-four ladies and two hundred *chapeaux* [gentlemen] were already assembled in the great hall. The ladies were seated on rows of raised benches. A concert was at once begun, during which an English ode, written in honor of the festival, was sung. This ode was composed of *ariettas*, recitations, and choruses. During the music, tickets were distributed to those of both sexes who desired to dance. Every *chapeau* received a ticket for a certain lady, with whom he was obliged to dance the entire evening, and which was numbered 1, 2, etc. During these dances, some distinction is made between the rank of the *chapeaux* and the ladies. Strangers, however, receive preference. Every couple goes through the minuet alone, and the ladies call off the name of the minuet to be danced. At large balls this custom becomes very tiresome. English dances are performed with two couples; and the long hall is divided off by rows of benches. All strife for precedence, or, in other words, *pushing*, is done away with; and the Governor himself, who is not a dancer, does everything in his power to keep things running smoothly. Ladies who do not care to dance put on a small *Bügel-Rocke;** and gentlemen who also do not feel like dancing, wear black cloth shoes with felt soles.

---

* Literally an "ironed cloak."

All kinds of refreshments were served ; and notwith-standing that the place was somewhat confined, no spectator was incommoded. The streets in front of the hotel were alive with people. At midnight a reg-ular supper was served at a number of tables. It is true that the eatables were all cold ; but delicacies and pastry could be had in superabundance. At 2 o'clock dancing was again renewed, and lasted until broad daylight. All the English, and the French officers of militia at Quebec gave these *fêtes*, which must easily have cost seven thousand *reich-thaler*.*

On the following morning, or rather the same morning (Jan. 1, 1777), the Governor held a *levée*, at which the Church, the Bar, the Army and Navy and commercial life were represented. The entire city fairly swarmed with *carioles*, for everybody was making New-Year's calls. We also made calls, but were obliged to refuse a number of invitations. In the afternoon we dined with M. de la Naudière ;† and in the evening there was a large assemblage at the Government-House, where play was kept up at about thirty tables till 10 o'clock, when every one went home

---

* A reich-thaler is about equal to seventy-five cents in U. S. money,

† Charles Louis Tarieu de Lanaudière. He accompanied his father-in-law, La Corne St. Luc, with a mixed band of Indians and Canadians, upon Burgoyne's expedition ; but he seems not to have taken a very prominent part in that campaign, and he returned to Canada before the capitulation. For a detailed sketch of him see *Hadden's Journal*.

and to bed. On the 2d we dined with Colonel St. Leger, colonel of the 34th Regiment and at present commandant at Quebec, and with whom we had become intimately acquainted while in camp at Chambly. As none but gentlemen were present, a large number of toasts were drunk.* In the evening, we asked permission of the General [i.e. Carleton] to return, notwithstanding we had been invited to several *fêtes*, and also to participate in a sleighing-party, made up of one hundred carioles, to the country-seat of Dr. ——. This man is a Doctor of Medicine, a Justice of the Peace, and uncommonly rich. He is the Lucullus of Quebec, and, like him, has no wife of his own.†

On Jan. 20th, Major-General von Riedesel celebrated the birthday of her Majesty the Queen at Three Rivers. We covered the distance (7 English miles) in four hours, in a cariole, and dined at a table laid for forty covers.‡ Many healths were drunk in cham-

---

* This must exactly have suited St. Leger, who liked a rollicking kind of life. See his performances in this line as related in the appendix to my " Sir John Johnson's Orderly Book."

† The reader will not fail to observe the subtle irony of this remark.

‡ General Riedesel, in giving an account of this dinner (see my translation, vol. i. p. 90), also says forty—a proof, incidentally, of the statement of the writer,—who appears to have been a person of unusual discrimination and accurate observation.

pagne, while, in front of the house, a small cannon was roaring ! A ball was given in the afternoon and evening, at which thirty-seven ladies were present. These remained to supper, and were waited on by their cavaliers. The charms of Demoiselle Tonnancour were greatly heightened by her jewels ; still, poor Demoiselle R——e, in her faded calico gown, was preferred by many, on account both of her natural and sweet charms, and the beauty of her voice. Know, my dear sir, that the Canadian beauties sing Italian and French *chansons ;* and also that numerous songs, composed in honor of General von Riedesel, have been sung in *Trois Rivières.*

I note the 5th of February as a great *fête*-day because, on that date, seven couples were married in the church at *St. Anne.* On this august occasion, the Brigadier led to the altar a niece of the *curé;* Major von Ehrenkrook, a squaw who was to marry an Indian of the Nation *des Fêtes de Boule ;* * and I, a relative of the Captain of Militia. This post of honor can only be filled when the intended brides have no fathers to give them away—their escorts, in such a case, taking the place of the latter. We dined with the *curé*, were entertained at the houses of the different brides, and

---

* "At Three Rivers the *Fêtes de Boule* tribe descended by the northern waters to this town, generally at the end of May or the beginning of June. Trade with this tribe was one of the principal industries of Three Rivers, and great efforts were made to direct it to the town."—*Kingsford's History of Canada.*

were the recipients of all those little attentions, courtesies, etc., which obtain among our peasants at home at a marriage-festival. As our musicians were in Quebec, and village musicians are unknown here, we were obliged to dance to the humming of the *tra-la-la* of a Canadian minuet. We also had to endure the bawling of *chansons*, sung from stentorian lungs. On account of our services to the brides, in giving them away, etc., we are considered by the good people of *St. Anne* as one of themselves; for, from the old grandmamma of 70 to the young maiden of 15 to 17 years, they all offer us their mouths to be kissed whenever they meet us. This is the Canadian greeting between relatives and intimate friends; more formal acquaintances offer merely their hands. This custom prevails not only among the well-to-do, but among the lower classes; and is one of the rights of friendship.

I have not heard from you for so long a time that I think your pen must be frozen. Therefore let *me* tell *you* something about Canadian snow. One of the damned disagreeable things to be met with in Canada is the prevalence of fierce winds. They rise generally every third day, and last about twelve hours. They cause the snow to drift from place to place, and gradually to fill up all the holes and pits until they are level with the rest of the land. The effect of this is to make the surrounding country look very pretty, but it is none the less dangerous to travel without taking proper precautions; otherwise one may tumble into one of these holes and break his limbs, or a horse and sleigh may fall into one and the horse remain buried alive for several weeks ! In the same manner as a forester and gun-master in our country can find a remedy for everything,* so these people over here know how to overcome all the difficulties incident to their roads in winter. Every *habitant* is compelled to keep the road clear between his own house and that of his nearest neighbor, to a width which will allow two *carioles* either to drive abreast or to pass each other. To facilitate this, young pine-trees are stuck up on each side of the road, twenty feet apart; and in this artificial alley one can drive with safety. One can scarcely imagine how these roads are changed, either by the weather or the force of circumstances; and each time a road is shifted it is renamed and the trees pulled up. The roads across the ice on the St. Lawrence River are staked out in a similar manner; and whenever a traveller meets with a weak spot in the ice, he is obliged to stop and mark the place. In fact, travelling in Canada is peculiar; for to-day the road may lead over a hill, and to-morrow over a river.

Pedestrians, however, can skim over the snow like hares by means of *raquettes* [snow-shoes], which they bind under their feet. These things are very similar to the *raquettes* we use at home to throw about a ball

---

* One of the duties in Germany of a forester or game-keeper is to keep the guns and all sporting articles in repair, and be a general *factotum.*

of feathers [a shuttlecock], the only difference being that they are twice as large. In using them, one must take a long stride, at the same time trailing his feet on a slant. The English regiments were busily engaged this last winter in learning to use them ; but our regiments have received none, as the required number have not yet been finished. Every *habitant* has such a machine,* which he cannot do without if he desires to promenade about the neighborhood.

Captain Foy † of the Royal Artillery, who occupies at the same time the position of Adjutant-General and Commissary of Musters, and who formerly commanded a company under Major-General von Rhetz in Germany, and an old acquaintance of yours, has a thorough knowledge of North America, having traversed it in all directions and looked at it critically,

---

* " These are undoubtedly the *scritofiuni* of Paul, the Longobard. See Ihre's *Glossarium* under the word *Skida*."— *Note by Schlözer*. Our word " skid " may also be derived from this word.

† Captain Eduard Foy—at this time *deputy* Adjutant-General, not Adjutant-General—resigned his position of Commissary of Musters June 6, 1777, when promoted to a full Adjutant-Generalship. He was appointed secretary of the Governor-General of Canada July 1, 1778, and died April 27, 1779. His wife accompanied Mrs. General Riedesel to Canada in the spring of 1777, when both ladies went to join their husbands. Regarding the reference to Germany in the text, it may be added that he served with distinction at the battle of Minden—receiving, the day after the battle, the thanks of Prince Ferdinand in General Orders.

with the eye of an engineer. He has been Governor of Hampshire [New Hampshire], and also has possessions in New England ; but since the Rebellion he has been compelled to look at both of them from afar ! Captain Phillips is really only a Lieutenant-Colonel of Artillery ; but, in this war, he has, by virtue of a royal commission, the place, rank and pay of a Major-General, by which title he is likewise designated. General Carleton, also, has the real pay, rank and honors of a General of Infantry, while in England he is but a Major-General.

We have now been sitting for four months in a veritable prison, cut off, as we are, from all communication with the neighboring States. We await, impatiently, the arrival of European ships, in order not only to obtain accurate news from Europe, but to find out what has been going on last autumn in New York, Jersey, Pennsylvania, and in our adjacent districts. Is that not sad ? The winter has been so mild that the streams in the wilderness of New Scotland [Nova Scotia] have not been frozen solid.* As a consequence, no one has been able to use the rivers as highways ; and even under the most favorable conditions of the ice, a single person cannot undertake a trip without risking his life a hundred-fold. In addition, the

---

* This open winter, at any rate, cannot be attributed either to the irrigation of the western deserts or the changing of the Gulf Stream ! As a general rule, I think it will be found that the climate of the United States and Canada is about the same, on the average, year after year.

St. Lawrence River, which seems to make ice for no other reason than to break it up, and which, furthermore, as if in sport, throws up masses of ice to the height of a mountain, only to let it come down with a crash like a house of cards, will allow no vessel to rest on its waters. Consequently, this highway is also closed to us. The rebels, who are still in possession of Carillon (which fort the Indians have rightly named Ticonderoga, or in French *Cul-de-sac*, because it lies in the *cul-de-sac* of Lake Champlain),* hem in all the news which otherwise might reach us by way of Albany, on the Hudson River, from our friends in the English North American States. Thus, there remains to us only one road by which we receive news, and this leads through the wilderness back of the English colonies, and lands one fifty miles the other side of Niagara. Anybody who is such a fool as to travel this road is of necessity compelled to hew for himself a path that may not again be trodden by human feet. We have actually received news by way of this road, although upon sifting it we have found it to consist of nothing save rumor. A very intimate friend of mine, Captain W—— of the 8th English Regiment, stationed for the last five years at Niagara, and in the smaller forts within a distance of 100 leagues from that post, but who, personally, has been attached to the German Corps, and upon all our marches and encampments

---

* The exact translation of the Indian name Ticonderoga is, " There the Lake [i.e. Lake Champlain] shuts itself."

has lodged with me, has, it is true, furnished me with news received from his comrades at Niagara. He has also sent the same to the dry and uninteresting newspapers at Quebec. Nevertheless, the particulars contained in these despatches lack confirmation. As yet, General Carleton has not received the least circumstantial or accurate information from the army of General Howe. This much, however, is certain, viz.: that the rebels have sustained severe reverses both at Long Island and at Kingsbridge. It is, moreover, confidently believed that a portion of Howe's army has entered Pennsylvania, and that the Quakers have withdrawn from Congress; also that Hancock and Franklin—two of the most important men in that body—have disappeared, and it is believed they have gone to Europe.* The quarters of General Lee, one of the foremost of the enemy's generals, have been broken up by a detachment of English light cavalry.

Our nearest foe, about 2000 strong, is stationed at Carillon, and is battling with want and misery. Our next expedition will be across† Lake Champlain to Carillon ; whence we shall probably march to Albany. Once there, we shall have the opportunity to get a look at New York, where many of our adherents, friends and countrymen are to be found. Mr. John

---

* This rumor was correct, so far as Franklin was concerned, he having arrived at the French Court on the 21st of December, 1776.

† It would have been more nearly correct to say *up* Lake Champlain.

MacKenna, an Irishman by birth, but raised at Löwen in the Netherlands and therefore half German, recently fled from a Catholic congregation in New York on account of disturbances there to our camp, and now preaches to the Catholic soldiers in the wilds of Canada, travelling from company to company. He has given me good descriptions of New York, and assures me that the larger portion of the law-abiding and prominent citizens of that town are royalists, but, for the present, are forced to remain passive.

The destruction of the enemy's fleet upon Lake Champlain has been a severe blow to them; and, accordingly, we have one less obstacle to overcome. Our operations will be mainly confined to ships; and, for this reason, every regiment will be supplied with twenty-five bateaux, which they will be compelled to row themselves. As soon as the river [Sorel] is open for navigation, we shall begin to drill our men, so that they can row either in divisions or in companies. The artillery is likewise mounted on bateaux which can quickly be collected so as to form batteries.

We have to adopt a peculiar method of warfare in this country—one entirely different from our system. In marching through forests and underbrush our infantry have to march two abreast, and at a distance of eighteen inches apart. Cavalry cannot be used at all, and our dragoons are therefore obliged to go on foot. Our standards are a great inconvenience, and none of the English regiments have brought theirs with them. Every English regiment has detached companies of grenadiers and light infantry, combined into battalions, which are very useful. The corps of Canadian Volunteers, under the command of Canadian officers, is not to be despised.

The Indians, on account of their inborn bestiality, are not to be trusted. They are very brave, but undisciplined ; and for this reason have English and Canadian officers. Now, however, they greatly desire to be independent, and, as faithful allies and friends, to fight for the king without being commanded by English generals and officers ; and an Iroke [Iroquois] named Joseph, who has spent some time in England and naturally knows something of the English and the savages, desires to achieve for himself a name as chief of an army of Indians.* Every means will be tried to prevent this ; for God help those colonists who are their near neighbors should this scheme be carried into effect !† The Indians are curious rogues who go from one extreme to another. I was in Loretto, [Lorette] where live that branch of the Hurons which more than eighty years ago embraced Christianity and have now become accustomed to cultivate their fields and raise cattle, and was astonished to see with what tenacity they still cling to the old customs of their

---

* Joseph Brant—Thayendanega. See Stone's *Brant*.

† As hinted at in the text, Carleton, who was an exceedingly humane man, undoubtedly used all his influence to curb the ferocity of the Indians. If the writer was alive the following year, he saw his prediction fulfilled in the Cherry Valley massacre by this same " Joseph."

ancestors. Their churches are very odd, and have neither chairs nor benches; but, on the other hand, they are filled with home-made wooden images of what, at one time, may have represented Hebrew, Greek, Roman or more modern European saints. Now, however, they are attired in savage costumes and have been beautifully daubed with paint. I will not soon forget the good St. Peter with his bunch of keys and his painted face!

I could give you still further droll accounts of the Indian Prince Athanas, revered by the savages within a radius of one hundred miles and who lives here, in Loretto; and also of his princes, his sons, and his three daughters, who are princesses. Prince Athenas, by the way, was cured of a wound in the leg by our Regimental Surgeon Br——, who since then is esteemed by the tribe as a veritable Æsculapius! But the sands in my hour-glass have nearly run; and so no more for to-night.

The 13th of April still finds us in our old Winter Quarters notwithstanding our preparations for marching were made three weeks ago. Everything in Canada depends upon the weather; and during the last four weeks its changes have been beyond belief. On the 5th and 6th of March we had a penetrating cold; the 7th was an agreeable spring day; from the 7th to the 16th we had a continuous thaw; and the days were so warm that all the ice-bridges on the great river (St. Lawrence) disappeared, causing General Carleton great difficulty in returning from Montreal to Quebec. From the 16th to the 20th the weather was disagreeable but not cold. On the 20th and 21st snow again fell to the depth of two to three feet. On the 25th it commenced snowing so violently that ice-bridges began again to form across the great river. Indeed, we have seldom had colder weather at home during Christmas week than we had here during Holy Week and the three Easter days. Great Northern Lights could be seen in the heavens every evening. On the 3d and 4th of April we again had a heavy snow-storm, and the cold was very severe. On the 5th it was moderately cold : during the evening of the 6th a heavy rain set in ; on the 7th we had several severe thunder-storms and a great thaw ; and on the 10th it was so warm that all the doors and windows were thrown open during the day, while in the night we had another terrific thunder-storm. The 11th, was raw and damp ; the 12th very windy ; and to-day, the 13th, the violent north-west wind which has been raging since sunrise has caused the weather to become so cold that it is almost impossible to keep warm in the room ; while everything is once more frozen as hard as a rock. How can an army cross rivers and march over execrable roads under such circumstances ?

The cracking of the ice in the St. Lawrence has been incessant all day. The violent wind has lashed the river into a fury, causing it to loosen huge cakes of ice which, after throwing them up into huge mountains, it again rends asunder. In spite of this, dear Brother, there are people who either voluntarily or from compulsion cross this river in canoes. The fact that two companies of Specht's regiment and one of Rhetz's, stationed in five parishes along the south side of the river, were obliged, in order to obtain their orders and provisions, to cross to the north side, has made it a burdensome affair for the regiments of the brigade. Thank God there have as yet been no accidents in our vicinity. Up to the present time of writing, God has spared us our health ; and in three weeks but one man has died in two regiments. Desertions are out of the question in Canada ; and no Canadian would think of helping a deserter along.

With our —— I have spoken several times both at Three Rivers and St. Anne, besides keeping up with him an uninterrupted correspondence. We have both taken great pains to make new discoveries and to study up Canada thoroughly. This, however, is extremely difficult ; and the stupidity and ignorance of the Canadians regarding their own country is beyond belief. To a certain extent, we already know more than they do ; and G—— will soon become so proficient that he will be able to send home a beautiful topographical map of Canada. The Grenadier Battalion lies about thirty leagues from us, on which account I have only been able to speak to two officers about it.

N. S.—We received news to-day (the 20th of April) that the English ship *London* had received orders to refit and sail for Europe as soon as possible. All letters must be finished immediately in order to get them to Quebec in time. I have already begun a new letter, which I will send by the next vessel, and in the course of the summer I intend writing you several. As the thaw has set in in earnest, we will, without doubt, begin our march in about ten days.

Several days ago Ensign von B—— was drowned in a stream no wider than the Ocker : how it happened I have not yet been able to learn. We have just received word that the brave Captain Mackay, with twenty-five Indians, has arrived here on his way to Quebec, having been for some weeks on a reconnoitring trip through the woods back of Crown Point and Carillon and as far as Lake Champlain. While on this scout, he dispersed a detachment of 16 officers and 23 men. Some of the members of his party also told us that a Hessian regiment has been surprised, half of it being captured and the other half killed.* On the other hand, everything seems to be going our way in Pennsylvania. It is also true that the rebels were badly whipped last year in New York and Jersey. On several occasions the Hessians are said to have massacred the enemy in a terrible manner. Neither would they give quarter, because the rebels refused to grant an exchange of prisoners.

Farewell.

---

* In allusion, probably, to the route of a Hessian regiment at Springfield, N. J., by Gen. George Clinton, Jan. 5, 1777.

LETTER FROM CASTLETON, VERMONT.

Castle-Town in New Hampshire.*

July 27, 1777.

We are now in a country called New Hampshire. It lies north of the old New England States, and is 100 to 150 English miles in length, by 50 to 40 in breadth. This country consists of so-called new Concessions [Grants], which, notwithstanding their name, have been in existence for more than eighty years. This tract of land is divided up into squares—6 to 8 English miles long and the same in width. The inhabitants seem to take delight in calling these sub-divisions Countries, Districts or Provinces. Then again, each of these squares is divided into sub-sections for habitations, and with such exactness that all boundary disputes in the future are precluded.† Each of these squares has a name and constitutes a small commonwealth of its own. It either has some rich man for

---

* The present State of Vermont.

† The writer in this remark was entirely mistaken, as witness the fierce and long dispute of the " New Hampshire Grants," between Vermont and New Hampshire.

seigneur, or is made up of free *habitans* who are very desirous of having a small market town or borough in their midst. It thus happens that often a name is given to a town when, as an actual fact, no such town is in existence. This is the case with Castle-Town which consists of about seventeen miserable houses. Clarendon, Grootland, [Rutland?] Pultney, &c., are neighboring counties. If you are desirous of obtaining a more lucid idea of this curious state of things, you will have to write to England for a map of the country called "The Province of New York, New Jersey, with a portion of Pennsylvania, and the Province of Quebec, drawn by Mayor Holland, 1777."

These "Concessions" [Grants] are not as thickly settled as they might be, since they are really the outskirts of the New England States. There is also a wide difference between the various counties in the way of population. In some, there are from forty to sixty houses; in others but twenty; and in still others only seven or eight. Many of them are but newly settled, and contain only a few straggling houses. Moreover, half, nay, perhaps two thirds or five sixths of these "Concessions," are entirely composed of summer *habitations* merely; for, in other words, the owners have built mere block-houses, having neither partitions, glass-windows, nor stoves. The probable reason for this is, that they live in them only from the beginning of spring until autumn. If the head of a house has numerous sons or daughters, he buys one of these places for a house, and either rents it himself in the spring, or sends some one of his family to it, who according to his instructions, destroys more and more of the trees upon it, until arable land, meadows and gardens are obtained. In this way, the land around his house increases in value yearly, until one of the sons or daughters marries, when it is presented to them. The young couple thus have a roomy and comfortable house to live in ; and from a merely summer habitation they convert it into a very comfortable home. Thoughtful fathers provide, in this manner, a substantial and permanent home for their children— situated, though they often are, fifty or more English miles from the old homestead. It so happens, therefore, that really elegant houses, well furnished, are often met with in this part of the country.

Very good grain, especially rye, is raised here ; and, indeed, the fields and meadows for the purposes of agriculture cannot be surpassed. The pasturage especially is so rich, that the Canadian cattle would become sick in feeding on it. It is true that the Canadian horses are fifty per cent better than those to be found here ; but, on the other hand, the horned cattle are eighty per cent better than those in Canada. The oxen here would lose nothing in comparison with those to be found in Friesland. They plow and pull heavy carts and wagons, in the construction of which no wood or heavy iron is spared. They (the oxen) pull them by the aid of a wooden yoke attached about their necks. The gardens are better and laid out on a more sensible plan than those in Canada ; and a lover of real, *genuine* trout ought to come to Castle-Town.

Many rattle-snakes are to be found in the woods in this vicinity ; and we have killed a number of them. Their bite is one of the most poisonous known. Death invariably follows within twelve hours, if the proper antidotes are not immediately taken, or unless the flesh around the bite is not at once cut out. As soon as a snake has been killed, some of the *habitans* present lose no time in cutting off the head and part of the tail and burying them in the ground ; as they believe that a pure and clear stream would be poisoned were the severed parts to be thrown into it. On one occasion, they begged of us a snake which one of our party had killed, and made of it a very palatable soup. In all seriousness, however, even the English regard the rattle-snake as a delicacy ; and prefer it to the best eel, especially if made into a soup, which is said to have a delicious flavor. These delicacies are extremely welcome in the kitchen of General Burgoyne. It may be that I am prejudiced, but none of it for me ! Thanks ! Recently, I had some green soup with Brigadier Fraser ; but of what it was made I do not know ; and perhaps if I had I might not have tasted it ! It was a turtle soup ; and now I know that *bouillon* can hardly have more strength or taste better !

The States of New York and New England are now engaged in a desperate lawsuit in regard to the ownership of the tract of land (where we now are)

called the "New Hampshire Grants." * I do not
wish to interfere in the matter or take sides ; therefore I am unable to state whether my feet at present
are resting on New England or New York soil!

In view of our difficulty with the rebels, as they
are called by the English, or with the "rebellers," as
they are termed by our people, it is probable that we
will have to appoint a day for a new term of court to
be held in the near future at Fort Edward, and
at which a decision will be given as to who shall
be master. Here [i.e. Fort Edward], for instance,
we have Mr. Putnam [Gen. Israel Putnam] stationed
with his corps. Fort St. George, on Lake George
(formerly called *Lac Sacrament*), is likewise occupied
by the rebels. American nuts !† Regarding the
sentiments of the various colonists, they vary in each
district. In Pultney the feeling is entirely in favor
of the rebels, and all the houses are empty. In
Castle-Town one third are royalists, and two thirds are
rebels. Clarendon is neutral, etc., etc. On an average, you may estimate that at the utmost one sixth
are royalists, one sixth are neutral, and four sixths
are rebels ; and in this computation I hardly believe

---

* If the reader is at all curious about this controversy, he
is referred to my "Life of Governor George Clinton" in the
"Magazine of American History" for June 1879, where the
subject is treated quite in detail.

† That is, "American nuts for us to crack"!—referring to
the problem of driving General Putnam and his corps from
Fort Edward, and the rebels from Fort George.

that I overestimate the numbers of the Americans (rebels).* Very few put themselves out to take the oath of allegiance, and numbers maintain a neutrality, very likely on account of our proximity and their possessions. In all truth, we are human and kind enough to these unhappy people. On the other hand, the rebels act in a harsh and barbarous manner toward those of their neighbors who manifest a friendly feeling toward us, and who have had the placards of an army placed upon their farms and houses in order to protect them.† As I said before, most of their houses are deserted, the inhabitants having fled into the interior with their goods and chattels. Consequently, any cattle that they have left behind them have become our lawful prizes. Thank Heaven we are no longer obliged to live on daily rations of pork and lard, for had we continued to live on these salt viands the consequences to our health in this heated climate would have been very pernicious.

The colonists, withal, are large, handsome, sinewy,

---

* This statement only corroborates how mistaken Lord George Germain was in planning the Burgoyne Expedition —thinking that all New England would flock to the Royal Standard. This has been fully and admirably brought out in Professor John Fiske's recent work on the "American Revolution."

† Undoubtedly the cruelties were not all on one side. Prof. Fiske, in his work above referred to, puts it correctly when he says: "There can be no doubt that Whigs and Tories were alike guilty of cruelty and injustice."

well built, strong and healthy men. The young women are white [i.e. fair], well formed and plump, and give promise of a numerous and healthy progeny.

You must know that there are many different sects in America who are distinguished from each other by their dress and their beards. It is a fact, that several of the inhabitants actually inquired of us as to what religion our grenadiers belonged; nor could they be made to believe that they all had one religion because they wore mustaches!

In the open field the rebels are not of much count, but in the woods they are redoubtable. At the present time we are almost continually marching through, and living in, forests. It is on such occasions that the rebels lurk in the woods and dart from tree to tree. In their skill as marksmen* they may be compared with our peasants in Sollinger: their riflemen are terrible. The latter wear a short white shirt over their clothes, the sleeves being bordered by a number of rows of white linen fringes. A rebel invariably looks for protection to his musket, which is very long. They load their guns with three small and three somewhat larger bullets; bad enough for him whom they hit. Nearly all of the wounded in the affair at Hubert-Town had three or four wounds—all caused by one shot. We have some consolation, however, in the fact that their muskets will not send a bullet farther than eighty paces; and they would

---

* Literally, " in their ability to hit an object."

find themselves in a sad fix if our soldiers could shoot as well as they. They respect, however, the prowess of our riflemen. From a military point of view, the officers of the rebels do not cut much of a figure; though an exception to this remark should be made in the cases of Captain Grobschmidt [Goldsmith?] Lieutenant Becker, Ensign Schneider, etc.—all tried men. You will also find that many of the privates in the American army are superior in station, in private life, to these superior officers; but in the above cases they evidently prefer military manœuvres to eating.

Our Indians, whom we brought with us from Canada, and who, while there, were supposed to be Christians, or nearly so, have since behaved like hogs. When it comes to plundering they are on hand every time;* and most of them have remained at Ticonderoga and Skeenesborough [now Whitehall, N. Y.]. While here they have filled themselves with rum in true military style. But few of their leaders remain true; and after every campaign they get "full," and remain in that condition until they reach home, when thay begin to brag of their deeds while away. The Indians who are attached to the corps of Colonel St. Leger are, on the contrary, of a better quality, but as yet we do not know where they are; perhaps we will

---

* An exact translation; in fact, the reader cannot fail to observe how many of our slang or, perhaps, idiomatic, expressions are the same both in German and English.

soon hear from them.*   A Mr. St. Luc has also 500 savages with him, which he has brought from distant northern countries.†   Among them are some Ona-toais.‡   The Onatoais have, hitherto, been bitter ene-mies of the English ; and in former wars dealt them many severe blows.   This is the first instance of their taking up arms for the English.§   These Indians are uncivilized, large-framed, warlike and enterprising, but as fierce as Satan.   They are accused of being canni-bals.   This, however, I do not believe, notwithstand-ing that they are capable of tearing their enemies to pieces with their teeth when infuriated.‖   In all prob-

---

* The writer to his chagrin probably heard very soon after-ward where both the Indians and St. Leger were—flying like stags before the hunters of the Mohawk Valley !   *Vide* Stone's "*Brant,*" and " Sir John Johnson's Orderly Book."

† In my " Orderly Book of Sir John Johnson," published by Munsell's Sons, Albany, N. Y., the reader, if he cares, will find the names of all these Indian nations under St. Luc. They, indeed, came from distant northern countries, coming from miles beyond the Great Lakes.

‡ Ottawas ; called also, by contemporary writers, Ottawa, Ottoauay, Ottoaua, Ottosa, Ottouaua.

§ And he might have added, through the influence of St. Luc, who was most shabbily rewarded for his services by the English Government.

‖ It remains, nevertheless, the fact, that the Indians—espe-cially the Ottauas—did practice cannibalism ; whether be-cause they fancied the flesh, or because they thought that to eat of the meat of their enemies it would make them brave. This is corroborated by proofs too numerous to mention.

ability there is no truth in the story that they keep a supply of human flesh on hand, for they seem to like the flesh of bullocks too well. Their carriage bespeaks their loyalty, and their savage decorations and ornaments become them quite well; indeed, their whole appearance is a soldierly one. Mr. St. Luc,* who is a Canadian himself, participated in several campaigns with them against the English during the last war (i. e., the war which lost Canada to the French), and in some respects became a terror to the English colonists.† He is still said to have a large number of English scalps in his possession. He is about sixty years of age, still very lively and active, and has only recently been released from his captivity among the rebels. He is rich. M. de La Naudiére, who is his son-in-law, has taken a command under him lately—a circumstance which astonishes me greatly.

I have just been agreeably surprised to receive your letters dated February 24th and March 2d. I have now received six letters in all from you during the present year. I have also, at this moment, received the joyful news that the ship "Isabelle Dorothea," with eighty-

---

The reader, however, is referred to Kip's "Early Jesuit Missions," where the writer furnishes from the narratives of the early Jesuit Fathers full proof of this statement.

* For an account of St. Luc see my "Burgoyne's Campaign," Appendix.

† St. Luc was the instigator of many of those forays on the New England settlements which kept that province in constant alarm and terror for so many years.

four recruits on board, and which had been given up for lost, has arrived safely at Quebec.

We have just parted from our beloved bateaux which brought us from Canada, and so safely carried us and our plunder over the St. Lawrence and Sorel * rivers and Lake Champlain, to our present place of abode. Our men have become good boatmen, and toward the last any bateau contained a good navigator [steersman]. The remainder of our voyage [journey] will henceforth be made on land. From necessity our baggage has been greatly reduced, and many officers will have nothing but their knapsacks. Horses, of course, are scarce and very dear, and those transports of horses that are gradually arriving from Canada will be used for drawing the cannon, magazine-wagons, etc. Nevertheless, I have two horses, and perhaps kind Providence will provide me with a third one. Most of the officers, also, have been able to secure at least one horse.

July 22d: The rebels have been polite enough to vacate Fort George. We are, consequently, finally masters of Lake St. Sacrement, a great advantage to us, as we can now bring up our provisions. They seem, however, inclined to lead us a dance about Fort Edward ; and we are, therefore, already beginning to brighten up our steps for the occasion.

On July 24th we marched to the Leading-Place

---

* The river running from Lake Champlain into the St. Lawrence, and also called the Richelieu and the St. John's.

[Landing-Place], and on the 25th to Skeenesborough. The English corps has advanced as far as Fort Anne,* and to-morrow we will follow them. The enemy has left Fort Edward. We intend to start for Albany, and to-morrow will send officers to Canada to hasten forward all of our recruits and other things that we left behind in that Province.

---

* It was while Burgoyne was at Fort Anne that the Jane McCrea tragedy occurred—a tragedy which in no way seems to belong to the dim past, when it is stated that Robert Ayers, the messenger sent to Jane by her lover, David Jones, was the father-in-law of the late Ransom Cook of Saratoga Springs. Mrs. Cook, who (1891) is still living, is the aunt of Mr. Nelson Millerd of New York City.

SENT AUG. 31, 1777, FROM THE CAMP AT DUAR HOUSE,* BY A NATIVE OF BRUNSWICK, SERVING IN BURGOYNE'S ARMY.

FORT EDWARD, Aug. 7, 1777.

The heat in this vicinity is uncommonly severe, and exceeds that of the warmest summer day in our own country. Almost daily we are visited by thunderstorms which, while being terrific, pass away very quickly and do not last as long as with us at home. They do not, however, cool the atmosphere after they are over; and in the night—more especially toward morning—there is such a heavy fall of due and mist, that it penetrates through our tents into our blankets even, causing them to become soaking wet.

On Aug. 9th Brigadier Fraser marched with his

---

* *Duer's House.* Built by, and the residence of, Judge Wm. Duer. He bought this property (at Ft. Miller,) from Gen. Ph. Schuyler. He married a daughter of Gen. Wm. Alexander, known as Lord Stirling in the Revolution. He was a delegate to the Continental Congress in 1777, and died in New York, May 7, 1799.

corps and the Indians toward Fort Miller. He, in turn, was followed by Colonel Baum with a separate corps, consisting of a regiment of dragoons and bodies of Indians, Canadian provincials, etc., and also several other detachments belonging to the brigades of Brigadiers Fraser and Specht, and the corps of Colonel Breymann. Colonel Baum took with him two English six-pounders under the command of Lieutenant Bach. Colonel Baum's object in making this march was to make a foray with 521 men into the now thickly settled districts of New Hampshire and the other old English provinces or so-called townships. It was hoped that by this movement our labors in obtaining provisions would not only be lightened, but, by collecting together the cattle remaining in the deserted homesteads of the rebels, and by buying the same from friendly farmers, we would have a fresh supply of provisions. At the same time, we expected to obtain horses and draught cattle, by means of which our army could advance with greater celerity. This, too, was the more desirable when it is remembered that our march had more than once been retarded by the arduous efforts of our soldiers trying to obtain even the smallest necessaries of life. In order to make this state of things clear to you, I would have to write pages. If, however, it be taken into consideration that the army, in these parts, eat bread composed of flour which has been prepared in England, also meat which has been salted in the same country, and that, before it can be put into pots and thence into our mouths, it has to be transported by men (because horses and carts are scarce in this country) over oceans, wide streams, large tracts of land, waterfalls, etc., it can readily be seen that to devise means to obtain these necessaries for the army is an undertaking of great responsibility for a commander-in-chief; more especially, also, is this the case if the commander-in-chief has to execute all these things in the face of an enemy—an enemy who must at once be driven, if possible, from any commanding position he may occupy, so as not to leave him to devastate his own lands to our detriment. Colonel Baum was accompanied by two English officers belonging to General Riedesel's suite, and also by Governor Skeene, who represented the commander-in-chief.* These three were to regulate all matters pertaining to the necessaries which we expected to find, in such a manner that no hue and cry could be raised by the Americans regarding atrocities.

On the 11th of August, a musketeer from Cologne, named Fasselabend, was placed in front of Riedesel's regiment and shot by the pickets belonging to the army. He had deserted, gone over to the enemy, and accepted their pay, but had been recaptured by us.

Aug. 12*th:* Brigadier Fraser is stationed on the Hudson River opposite Saratoga. General Arnold, of the enemy's forces, is at Stillwater.

---

* That is, *Burgoyne:* and it would have been greatly to the advantage of that general had he had nothing to do with General Skeene. See "Burgoyne's Campaign" and "Ramsay's Revolutionary War."

Aug. 13*th :* Colonel Breymann and his grenadiers, together with a battalion of riflemen (yagers), broke camp and started on a march for Fort Miller. Colonel Baum has begun his march toward the neighborhood of Bennington.

Aug. 14*th :* The army to-day marched seven English miles down the Hudson, and encamped at Fort Miller. Rhetz's regiment marched from Jones's House toward Fort Edward ; and the Hessian-Hanau Regiment from Fort Anne to Jones's House—thus occupying our old quarters. Brigadier Fraser has crossed the Hudson and now lies at Saratoga. Colonel Breymann, on the other hand, still remains on this side of the river opposite Saratoga. It was terribly warm to-day, and many of the men ran the risk of being suffocated while on the march. Fort Miller is situated on the other side of the Hudson [i.e. left bank] and is entirely in ruins. It never, indeed, consisted of more than a block-house and a magazine surrounded by palisades. The army is now encamped at DUAR'S HOUSE. Mr. Duar [Duer] is a member of the rebel Congress and also commissary of the army. His country-seat here is built of wood, but is large and tastefully arranged. It is the first real country-seat that I have seen since my departure from Portsmouth.

Aug. 15*th :* Colonel Breymann was obliged to march to the assistance of Colonel Baum, twenty-five English miles distant. He took with him two English 6 pounders, under the command of the Hesse-Hanau, Lieutenant Spangenberg. Colonel Breymann left his camp in the same condition as the dragoon regiment, which left its tents, baggage and standards behind.

Aug. 16*th :* A bridge was thrown across the Hudson, and the army received orders to proceed on their march [to Albany] the following morning.

Aug. 17*th :* During the night, or rather toward daybreak, Capt. M. de Lanaudière, who had left us with Baum's corps, arrived with the news that Baum's corps had surrendered at discretion to the enemy, at St. Coick's Mill, not, however, without a desperate resistance, nor until all their powder had been shot away. Yesterday afternoon, and before Colonel Breymann could come to their assistance, the enemy, who was estimated at about 4000 men, attacked Baum's corps on all sides.   Baum had intrenched himself with his regulars on an elevation, as well as time and circumstances would permit.   These troops consisted of his dragoon regiment, not more than 150 men strong, and the infantry detachments that had been sent along with him.   He was thoroughly convinced (mark you) that Colonel Breymann was marching to his assistance, and he, therefore, resolved to hold his position that he might not loose any of his cattle, horses and flour—the great objects for which he had been sent by Burgoyne on this foray—and which he had already accumulated before the battle.   The country people of the neighborhood not only had accepted the proclamation of General Burgoyne, but had gone in crowds to Governor Skene, and taken the oath of loyalty to the king. But these same disloyal people, who had just taken the oath of allegiance, soon afterward attacked the corps of Baum as the bitterest of foes. Meanwhile, a strong detachment of the enemy's regulars from Stillwater had incited the inhabitants within a radius of twenty-four English miles and more, to arm without exception. These suddenly came out of the woods from all sides. The Indians, Canadians, and Provincials were dispersed, and Colonel Baum attacked with fury on all sides. Eye-witnesses have asserted that the rebels on this occasion fought with desperation, advancing to within eight paces of cannon loaded with slugs, so that they might more easily shoot down the artillerymen. The defence of Colonel Baum was equal, apparently, to such an attack ; for three times the enemy were forced to retreat before his fire. At last, however, the cartridges were exhausted, and Baum's two cannon silent from lack of powder. At this vital moment, the enemy threw themselves fiercely upon our men ; and Baum and his dragoons, sword in hand, and the infantry with their bayonets, endeavored to hew a path through the enemy's lines into the woods. But, alas ! at this point the narrative ceases ; and up to the present moment we are still uncertain as to the fate of our brave brothers. Many are perhaps dead ; still more wounded ; and the rest are in the hands of the enemy.

The commanders of the above-mentioned light troops belonging to Baum's corps, have all saved themselves with the exception of a certain Lieutenant

Sallans of the 9th English regiment, and a Swede by birth, who is dead. One hundred and twenty-seven men belonging to the infantry of the German regiments are missing, and their fate is uncertain. We expect, within a short time, to hear more accurate details ; and many are, without doubt, still living. Counting the well and sick dragoons, and also the recruits from this regiment, over eighty men are still fit for duty.

Through this same bearer of evil news, M. de Lanaudière, we have also learned that, soon after the first unlucky affair, Colonel Breymann also became engaged in a heated affray with the enemy ; but as to the termination of which he can tell us nothing. As one verified dispatch after another reached us, to the effect that Colonel Breymann was retreating safely, the army remained encamped on the river Battenkill.* Burgoyne and the 47th Regiment, however, waded through the river, and marched to meet Breymann. Toward 4 o'clock Breymann's corps arrived in the camp, greatly fatigued by the engagement, the heat of the day, and their forced marches. It appears that yesterday afternoon, about 4 o'clock, Breymann arrived at St. Coick's Mill, and saw the enemy stationed upon an eminence. He was not then aware that anything serious had happened to Baum's corps. He had, however, learned from a dragoon on horseback,

---

* This is not a river, but merely a large stream, which empties into the Hudson, almost opposite the present " Marshall House," the place described by Mrs. Riedesel.

that Baum was in great danger.* Accordingly, with his two battalions, he lost no time in advancing rapidly upon the enemy ; attacked furiously ; dislodged them successively from three different eminences in the woods, and forced them to retreat to a distance of a mile. However, the numerical superiority of the enemy, together with constant reinforcements from the neighboring villages, and finally the scarcity of powder and ball, obliged his seemingly victorious corps to retreat. This was made in safety. The cannon, however, owing to all the horses having been killed, were left behind. From the fact that this engagement took place in a dense woods, with thick underbrush, we at present do not know our actual losses. Many of our wounded were of necessity left behind. One captain, one lieutenant, and fourteen men are dead. This we know to be a certainty. Lying wounded in the hospitals, are one major, two captains, one lieutenant of the Rifles, one lieutenant of the Artillery, and sixty-three men. The wounded are in a tolerable condition and most of them will again be fit for service. The fate of five officers and one hundred and thirty-five men who are missing is unknown. Colonel Breymann, whose coat was pierced by five bullets, received a flesh wound upon his left leg, notwithstanding which he remained with his corps. This evening he again took possession of his old quarters, and the army re-occu-

---

* This statement is rather singular when it is remembered (see "Burgoyne's Campaign") that Breymann had been sent to the rescue of Baum by Burgoyne.

pied their old camp.   Fraser's corps, however, took
up a position on the Battenkill river.

Aug. 18*th:* General Riedesel advanced with the
47th Regiment to Jones's House, and the regiment of
Rhetz and Hesse-Hanau, with a train of artillery,
did the same.   This movement was made for the purpose of covering Fort George, whence, at very great
inconvenience, we have to bring all our provisions
and other necessary articles for the army.   This has
kept us busy up to the present time, during which we
have remained in peaceful possession of our quarters.
Many Albanians have come to us, and very soon we
will have an entire regiment of Provincials.   Over
five hundred horses have also arrived from Canada.
Colonel St. Leger has captured Fort Stanwix on the
Mohoc [Mohawk] River,* and will soon join his forces
to ours, and advance upon the enemy.   Lord Cornwallis, also, is on the march with a corps of Howe's
army, and both armies [Burgoyne's and Howe's] will
strive to effect a junction.   The unfortunate occurrences at St. Coick's Mills have not dampened our ardor.
We regret nothing except the loss of brave friends
and men.   This small piece of good luck has cost the
enemy dear, and they have learned to know the worth
of their foe.   They did not dare to follow Colonel
Breymann more than a quarter of a mile.   The grenadier companies of Rhetz and Specht must have been

---

* Of course a mistake.   On the contrary, St. Leger had to
beat a hasty and ignominious retreat.

in the thickest of the fray during the retreat, since they have the largest number of officers and men missing. To fight in desolate forests and thick underbrush is ticklish work; and one company in advance of another, can easily become fortunate or unfortunate.

Aug. 27th: A deserter from the 9th English Regiment was shot before the whole camp. It is true that deserters are treated with great severity; but it is also true that up to the present time there has never been an army in which desertions have been so scarce. You must also bear in mind that the enemy, through its emissaries—who are partly of English and partly of German extraction—is trying, by every means in its power, to induce our soldiers to desert.

But, dear friend, when shall you hear again from me, and when shall I again receive news from you? Mother Canada has given her children their dowries, and from her we need expect nothing more. We must get our living by the strength of our arms, and with them hew a path which will lead us to it either in the neighborhood of our friends or enemies, or have it brought to us across oceans and seas from Europe. Such will probably be the case with our correspondence. So do not be astonished if a long time elapses ere you again receive a letter from me. May the winds soon waft joyful tidings to you over the sea; and by the same means may they convey good news to me of your continued prosperity and your faithful remembrance of your friend.

A PRIVATE LETTER FROM NEW ENGLAND, NOV. 15, 1777, TO OCT. 10, 1778.*

My Dear Friends:

At last we have arrived at Cambridge, where we poor unfortunates can claim neither to be free nor captives. If I were to write and tell you that every thing is as it should be here I would be stating a base falsehood. However, if I wished to excite your sympathy to the highest pitch by my complaints, I fear I should afterward regret the tears I should cause to flow. The Americans, who, for politeness sake, are no longer termed Rebels or Yankees, are very often unable to determine to which class of people in

---

* As is well known, Burgoyne's defeat at Saratoga changed the whole complection of affairs for the colonists. This great event is here described even to the most minute details by an eye-witness, who has the great faculty of making the reader imagine himself an eye-witness of these stirring events.—*Note by Schlözer.*

their state we properly belong.* It is true that we are somewhat confined. As a matter of fact, we are allowed a well defined circle, the bounds of which we are not to overstep under penalty of being sent to the prison-ship or shot. We, however, make the most of the little liberty we possess in our villages of palisades, and now and then play the gentleman among our conquerers.

You are doubtless very anxious to know exactly how we arrived at the High School of Cambridge where the students live in the well-built *Collegio Harvardino;* attend college in comical-looking dressing-gowns, and are summoned three times daily to breakfast, dinner, and supper, by the sound of a bell. Paper and ink, however, are too dear in this place, to go into minute details of occurrences from the 1st of September up to the present time. I will, however, do the best I can. Speaking confidentially, I cannot tell you how it was that we got here and into this predicament, for it is a subject that has caused much thinking, speaking, and writing, and will, doubtless, cause much more of the same. But you may take my word of honor for it, and rest assured that it was neither the fault of the army nor its behavior ; and, further, that, notwithstanding the reverses, we are still able to meet the gaze of our still more successful comrades

---

* The writer's meaning is not quite clear. Perhaps his idea is that they are unable to classify the prisoners according to their social position.

with courage and confidence. For a similar reason the army cannot accuse its commander-in-chief. On the contrary, it believes that he will eventually right himself before his king, his country, and the rest of the world. Perhaps the story of our march over seas, rivers and mountains, and through forests and wildernesses will cause our successors either to forego it, or to make other preparations before undertaking the same journey. For the latter purpose, our experiences can furnish a small practical text-book.

My last letter to you ended with a description of the unfortunate affair at Bennington, and since then we have been unable to send even a line to Europe. Notwithstanding that we have the wide ocean, which furnishes us with oysters, shell and other fish, close at hand, and notwithstanding, also, that this same ocean still affords us the means of communication, I am unable to know whether this letter, which I have written to my friends on the Ocker, will reach them. If I had had my say when the articles of capitulation were drawn up, I would have seen to it that the safe forwarding of letters was embodied in a 14th article. The wiseacres, however, have only put into the Convention treaty *thirteen* articles—one it would appear for each Province.* Since last April my eyes have read no letter of yours. The wine which you so kindly sent me from Lower Saxony, actually got as far as Caril-

---

* As our writer says, The Convention treaty consisted only of thirteen articles.

lon, on Lake Champlain, but it could not be transported over the wretched thirty-six miles from that post to Fort George—at which place, had it come, we would gladly have unloaded it, notwithstanding the terrible heat of the weather; and so I was forced to forego the pleasure of drinking it.

In the affair at Bennington those actually killed were Colonel Baum, Reineking, master of the horse; Captain von Schieck, Lieutenant Mühlenfeldt, and Hagermann, color-bearer. Lieutenant d'Annieres, Jun., died of dysentry a few days afterward in captivity. Lieutenants Breva and Gebhard are severely wounded and prisoners. Cornet Stretzer, Color-bearer Specht, and Chaplain Melsheimer* are slightly wounded and prisoners. Major von Bärner and Lieutenant Hannemann managed to escape, but were so severely wounded that they had to be brought back to Canada. Colonel Breymann and Captains von Geusau and Von Gleissenberg were wounded—the latter severely. Those who managed to escape without wounds but were captured, are Major von Meiburn, captain of horse, Von Schlagenteufle, Jun., Captains von Bartling, Sen., Dommes and O'Conell, Lieutenants von Reckrodt, Von Bothmar, Meyer and Burghoff, and the cornets and color-bearers Gräff, Schönewald and Andra. Those officers are in the vicinity of Westminster [Vermont], and are divided up among the various farm-houses.

---

* Chaplain Melsheimer afterward deserted to the Americans. I have his journal, a very rare work, which I have recently translated for the Quebec Historical Society.

This affair was to us a severe blow. It caused us to halt in the midst of a successful march. The magazine at Bennington escaped our outstretched hands; and we were therefore again obliged to fall back upon our stores of flour and salt meat stored at Fort George. Meanwhile our army remained encamped at Duar's House, and Major-General von Riedesel was forced to take up his position with a corps at "Jones's House." All our regiments were now engaged, though without interruption, in the difficult task of bringing up the necessaries for the remainder of the campaign in boats. It was, moreover, very laborious work to get around the rapids between Fort George and Saratoga by the carrying-places, on account of the scarcity of carts and horses. My dear sirs, only think of it! It was August, the hottest time of the year, when, although sitting quietly in our tents, we could hardly draw breath. The dysentery was also causing fearful havoc among us; and notwithstanding it all, we were obliged to work like beavers, since the very life of our army depended on our doing so. Indeed, I really believe that in honor of our misfortunes a stone will hereafter be erected between Ticonderoga and Albany, with this inscription: *Vestigia me terrent!*

Enough time was gained by the enemy by their lucky *coup* at Bennington to allow three brigades to join them, General Gates, the favorite of the New Englanders, assuming the command.* The farmers left

---

* The reason why Gates—that malicious and cowardly intriguer—was at this time the favorite of the New Englanders,

their ploughs, the blacksmiths their anvils, the shoemakers, tailors, etc., their several vocations, and came
as volunteers ; while from all the provinces of New
England regiments of militia came swarming in to
join the forces under General Gates. Thus within
fourteen days the force of the enemy was augmented
to 14,000 men. Meanwhile General Arnold was sent
against Colonel St. Leger, who was on the point of
capturing Fort Stanwix on the Mohawk River. The
rumor that our entire army had been defeated at Bennington had already travelled in advance of Arnold ;*
and this, in connection with the fact that St. Leger
found his position none too favorable, caused him to
raise the siege and return to Oswego.

General Burgoyne now resolved to concentrate his
army and give battle to the enemy, who had already
advanced from Stillwater. This determination gave
great satisfaction and enthusiasm in the army. All
articles that could be dispensed with were sent back to
Diamond Island in Lake George. It is for this reason
that I am now wearing a ragged coat and most pitia-
ble-looking shirts. However, the same state of things
exists with all of us.

---

was because he had, with a view of supplanting Schuyler of
New York, lost no opportunity of offensively declaring that
the Government of New York was entirely wrong in the
matter of the New Hampshire Grants. See Fiske's "American Revolution," where this fact is fully brought out.

* A new fact.

On the 11th of September our entire army made a still further advance against the enemy.

On the 13th, 14th, and 15th we crossed the Hudson on a bridge of boats—the enemy meanwhile falling back upon Stillwater. And now we had again a repetition of salt meat and flour for our diet. My dear friends, do not despise these royal victuals, the cost of the transportation of which from England must have been a right royal sum. Pork at noon, pork at evening, pork cold, and pork warm! Friends, you who at home are able to dine upon green peas and shell-fish, might have looked down upon our pork with disdain; for us, however, pork was a kingly viand, without which we would have starved. In fact, if we had had pork enough we would not now be here in Boston.* Our hospital was forced to follow us, otherwise the enemy would have captured it. All communication with Lake George and Carillon, and consequently with Canada, now ceased.

On the 15th of September we took up a position at Dovogat's House; regaled ourselves once more with excellent vegetables, and slept upon straw, large heaps of which were to be found in the neighboring fields. That it had not been threshed did not materially affect our comfort. This good fortune was the first of the kind we had experienced in America, and we appreciated it.

---

* That is, if the supplies even of pork had not given out, Burgoyne would not have surrendered.

On the 16th, several regiments started upon a reconnoitring expedition, and also to repair ruined bridges
and roads ; and on the 17th, we advanced two and a
half English miles to Soarts' [Swords'] House.*

On the 18th, the enemy seemed inclined to dispute
our right to repair a number of bridges ; and finally we
were obliged to send out entire regiments to cover our
workmen.

On September 19th, both armies encountered each
other in a swamp. The neighborhood, which consisted of wooded knolls, ravines, morasses, etc., was the
cause of amazing mistakes on both sides. On account
of these obstacles the several columns of our army presented to the enemy a front of the width of two and
one half English miles. The left wing, consisting of the
German regiments, all the heavy artillery, and the 47th
English Regiment, under the command of Major-General von Riedesel, had no hand in the first engagement, because they were marching along the river flats.
Our grenadiers and light-infantry battalion, which to-

---

* A son of the Swords who built this house was for many
years a respected bookseller in New York City. There is
a tablet now in existence in Trinity Church, New York, in
the alcove of the Astor Memorial, south side, and which was
erected by Trinity Church corporation, bearing this inscrip-
tion : " In Memory of | Thomas Swords | who was for fifty
years an eminent | Publisher and Bookseller in this city | and
for twenty-five years a vestry | man of this Church | Born in
| Fort George, Saratoga Co., N. Y., | January 5, 1764.
| Died in this city | June 27, 1843."

gether with Fraser's corps formed the right wing, took
part in the conflict.   Colonel Breymann, in particular,
had the honor to strike the enemy's flank, which had
hemmed in the 24th English Regiment, with such force
that they speedily withdrew.   Colonel Breymann, who
by this movement had again established communication between Fraser's corps and the rest of the army,
gained special laurels.   His battalion also lost but few
either in killed or wounded.   Towards three o'clock in
the afternoon, our centre, consisting of the 9th, 20th,
21st, and 62d English regiments, under the command
of Brigadier Hamilton, became fiercely engaged with
the enemy.   The firing still continuing, Captain of
Artillery, Johnson, supported the English brigade with
a brigade of artillery ; and, at the same moment, that
old veteran, Major Williams, with many groans and
curses, also brought up several of his "thunderers" from
over the hills.   The enemy, on the other hand, brought
up fresh brigades one after another.   Hamilton's brigade maintained itself bravely ; and notwithstanding
it had been forced several times to retreat, it again
advanced and victoriously occupied its former position.   Finally, General Burgoyne sent word to General von Riedesel, on the river bank, to send as
many troops as he could spare from the left wing to
the assistance of Hamilton's brigade.   Thereupon
General Riedesel, turning over the command of the
left wing to Brigadier Specht, and leaving the latter to
oppose the already advancing front of the enemy, took
with him two companies of Rhetz's regiment under

command of Captain Fredersdorf, and two 6-pounders under the command of Captain Pausch of the Hesse-Hanan artillery, and hastened to the relief of Burgoyne. He reached Hamilton's brigade when it was in its last struggles and upon the point of retreating. He at once fell upon the enemy's flank with great success, Captain Pausch at the same time raking them with a murderous fire of grape. The result was, that the English regiments, being thus infused with fresh courage, re-formed themselves, and with loud hurrahs threw themselves furiously upon the enemy. The latter fled and left us in possession of the battle-field, acknowledged victors. The sun soon afterward went down, and night hid the flying enemy from our view.*

The action of to-day has caused the house of a poor farmer to become famous ; for it has given to this day's engagement the name of the " Battle of Freeman's House." † None of the officers belonging to our Ger-

---

* When it is stated that Riedesel, Pausch, the writer of this letter, and other reliable eye-witnesses all concur in saying that the Germans saved the fortunes of this day, it seems almost incredible that Burgoyne, neither in his despatches nor subsequently in his explanations before Parliament, should scarcely have mentioned Riedesel and his help. If it sprung from petty jealousy, it was unworthy of Burgoyne, who, whatever his failings as a military man, bore a character for highmindedness.

† Afterwards known as the " Battle of Freeman's Farm." Connected with this Freeman's farm is a rather curious incident. A Michael Condon, who died this year (1891), was

man corps was killed or wounded, and of its men only eighteen were either wounded or killed. The 62d English regiment, however, suffered severely ; for out of 300 of its men who went into the action, three officers, one under-officer, and forty-nine privates were killed, and eight officers, nine under-officers, and ninety-two men wounded. Ten of the English officers were killed, among whom were the brave Captain of Artillery, Johnson, and Captain Monnin of the Canadian Volunteers, whose eleven-year son had fought by his side.* Our poor wounded were brought down to

---

in his youth a day-laborer on this farm. He had been set to work digging ; and when, at noon, the owner of the place came along, he found a post-hole dug in the ground, in which there were yet one or two gold pieces scattered around. These, as the owner of the farm, he claimed and took. A year afterward Condon bought and *paid for* a very expensive farm in the vicinity, which is known to this day as "The Battle Farm ;" and while no one could say positively that it was bought with gold that he had secreted, yet none doubted the fact. Burgoyne's treasure-chest, if the gold came from that, was therefore of some benefit !

* In this connection it will be of interest to mention that probably the *last survivor* of this action was Colonel George Williams, a nephew of Major Griffith Williams (mentioned in the text) who commanded on this occasion Burgoyne's artillery. He was a cadet at the time (see General Rogers in *Hadden's Journal* for the duties and pay of cadets, p. 156), and was but twelve years of age—but one year older than Captain Monnin's son. This youngster is said to have carried the flag of truce into the American lines on the capitulation of Burgoyne. At the end of the American War he

the low ground on the river-bank. No houses were near at hand to carry them into, nor did we have help enough to tie up their wounds.* There was no help for it, therefore, but for them to remain in the open air during the entire night (which had become bitterly cold and freezing) until the next day, when tents were put up for their use. This experience constitutes a truly American evil, for which there appears to be no remedy.†

On the 20th of September we took up a position as near as possible to the enemy's intrenchments, in which they had now ensconced themselves, being separated from them by forests and ravines.

On the 21st, the enemy decidedly objected to our hewing paths through the forest to our advanced out-

---

joined H. M. 20th Regiment, and served with it for twenty-three years in Jamaica, St. Domingo, and Holland, and also on the staff of General Crampagne in Ireland during the French invasion of 1798. He represented Aston in the first reformed Parliament, and died at Little Woolton, near Liverpool, in 1850, at the age of 88. See " Forty Years in Ceylon." By the late Thomas Skinner. London, Allen & Co. 1891." I am indebted to my warm friend John J. Dalgleish of Edinburgh, Scotland, whose grandfather served under Burgoyne, for bringing these facts to my notice.

* The writer is hardly correct here. There were two small log-houses, and one frame one of two rooms, in the latter of which General Fraser died. See my translation of Madame Riedesel's letters.

† The writer means, I suppose, that no way had yet been found to supply hospital facilities.

posts. This gave rise to several skirmishes, which, however, did not amount to much. From this time on we turned out every morning an hour before day-break to enjoy the morning air, which was composed partly of hoar-frost, and partly of a mist so dense that you could in very truth grasp it with your outstretched hands. Nor did it entirely disappear before nine o'clock in the forenoon. During the day it was hot enough to melt one. We intrenched our quarters, placed all our guards and pickets in a circle around our camp, and protected them by means of redoubts and batteries. In the rear of our camp we also placed two large re-doubts for the protection of our magazines, trains, and hospitals.* In a word, our encampment was a copy of that at Croffdorff in 1759. Then we cut down several thousand trees, not only to give our cannon more play-room, but also to increase the efficiency of their range. Soon we began to feel the scarcity of many articles. We could not obtain anything from Carillon, nor in this wilderness could anything be had; while, to make matters still worse, the enemy had cut off all means of communication with Albany. One bottle of poor red wine cost 2 reich-thaler and 8 groschen of our money [$1.58], and a pound of sugar or coffee was worth one reich-thaler and 22 groschen

---

* These two redoubts on two high elevations by the river-bank (in one of which Fraser was buried) are to be seen in the picture—taken from *Anbury*, much reduced—in Lossing's "Field-Book of the American Revolution" and in my "Bur-goyne's Campaign."

[97 cts.]. Clothes were not to be thought of, for they were daily torn into shreds in this wilderness. At no time did the Jews await the coming of their Messiah with greater expectancy than we awaited the coming of General Clinton. This officer General Howe was supposed to have sent us for the purpose of dispersing the rebels in our front and rear. Flying rumors from time to time reached our camp in regard to his army; and although they continually filled us with renewed hope, they proved, alas! to be nothing but rumors. The enemy, meanwhile, had sent an expedition against Carillon under the command of General Lincoln, which surprised and captured four companies of the 53d Regiment. Lincoln, however, was driven back from Carillon and Diamond Island with great loss, so that he was defeated in *optima forma.* Our provisions continued to decrease; the soldiers were reduced half a pound of bread and the same quantity of meat per day—a state of things which they endured with patience. Meanwhile, although the enemy had it in their power to attack us with four times as many men as we had, they showed no inclination to do so. To retreat seemed too hard lines for General Burgoyne. In Albany we had plenty of friends willing to reinforce us; and for this reason the General resolved to attack the enemy and endeavor to force his way through their lines. We could only attack the enemy on their flank; and in order to hew a way for our columns and artillery, and at the same time reconnoitre their position, an expedition of 1500 men under command of the several leaders of the army, with a number of heavy cannon, was undertaken on the 7th of October.

Generals Burgoyne, Phillips, and Riedesel, and Brigadier Fraser, accompanied the expedition, and all the different regiments of the army contributed their quota. The brigadiers and those troops that remained in the rear retired behind the fortifications of the camp in order to be in a position to defend themselves as strongly as possible should the enemy take a notion to attack them. Toward three o'clock in the afternoon the enemy were driven from several positions, and the corps marched up to Weisser's House.* The enemy meanwhile remained quiet, being hidden from view by woods. General Burgoyne was on the point of continuing the reconnoissance, when suddenly, about four o'clock in the afternoon, the enemy threw themselves upon the English grenadiers who composed the left wing, attacked them in front and in flank, and forced them after a stubborn resistance to give way.

---

* This does not describe the state of affairs exactly. From this sentence it might be inferred that the main body of the enemy "were driven," etc.; whereas, if any were forced to retire, it was only a few pickets. The entire army of Gates remained in their intrenchments until the attack on Burgoyne was determined on. Pausch, in his *Journal*, speaks of coming up to this house and finding it deserted—it having been occupied, probably, as an outpost by a few American pickets. In connection with this, the reader is referred to "Stone's Map of the Battle-ground" in that *Journal*.

At the right wing, where the regiments under English commanders were placed, the same thing happened ; and simultaneously the centre, under Colonel von Specht, and whose flanks were no longer covered, was also attacked.   The centre stood its ground for a long time ; but as the enemy's regiments kept pouring in from all sides, nothing was left to it but to retreat.   A more galling discharge of musketry could not be imagined.   Captain Pausch of the Hesse-Hanau artillery afterward described to me with what frenzy the enemy threw themselves upon his cannon, in the very teeth of a murderous fire of grape.   Although Captain Pausch's desperate courage in such affairs is well known, yet he does not wish on that account that his " Narrative" should be taken as an excuse for the loss of his two 12-pounders.   Old Major Williams, who can only be likened to an old 12-pounder himself, and who adores no creature on earth more than a 12-pounder,—and none, by the way, can handle one better than him,—also met with Captain Pausch's fate ; with this difference, however, that he was captured along with his beloved 12-pounders.*   The old warrior is said to have shed tears upon this occasion.   The result of to-day's unfortunate engagement was that nearly all of our cannon were captured, and the entire detachment had to seek safety in flight.   The beaten corps took refuge within the large intrenchment [the

---

* It was one of these same twelve-pounders on which Col. Cilley was a-straddle and exulting in its capture as described by Wilkinson.

" Great Redoubt"] of Fraser's division, and although the enemy attempted to scale and enter it, they were met with such a determined resistance that all their efforts proved vain.

We were, however, to meet with another misfortune. Bellona seems to have been with the Yankees to-day, and Mars must either have been in a bad humor or have placed too much confidence in old Williams and his 12-pounders. The corps of Fraser and Breymann were separated by a ravine, and both were stationed upon two separate knolls. The low ground between these elevations, and on which Freeman's house lay, was occupied by Canadians and Provincials. Colonel Breymann's corps covered the entire right of the army, and therefore stood *en potence.* The Provincial and the Canadian corps had given their quota to the reconnoissance of the morning ; and the grenadiers and rifle battalion had, moreover, become greatly weakened by the affair at Bennington. This entire division therefore mustered scarcely two hundred men. The defeated corps, likewise, instead of throwing a portion of its men into Breymann's intrenchment, threw them all into Fraser's.* Colonel Breymann was attacked in front, and defended himself bravely.

The enemy, however, overpowered the posts in the depressed ground between the two knolls, and then threw themselves from the side and rear upon Brey

---

* Still, if the defeated corps had divided up its strength, Fraser's " Great Redoubt" would probably have been taken —thus making the general result of the day the same.

mann's intrenchments. Breymann fell dead as he stood near two cannon. His corps became dispersed, the greater part of them, however, retreating into the forest, and afterwards effecting a junction with Fraser's division. The enemy captured several cannon, set the tents on fire, and plundered the camp. Colonel Breymann, as before mentioned, and several other officers of the German corps, were killed. My esteemed old friend Captain Fredersdorff died some time afterwards from his wounds, and Lieutenant and Adjutant Bode met with the same fate. Captain von Dahlstjerna received a dangerous shot through his right leg, causing both arteries to be ruptured. He is lying at Albany, and it is to be hoped that his recovery will be speedy.* Captain von Gleissenberg was also dangerously wounded in the stomach ;† and Lieutenants von Meyer from Nuremberg and Cruse of the Yägers [riflemen] only slightly. Ensign von Geyling, of the Hesse-Hanau Regiment, is killed ; and Colonel von Specht, Captain von Geisnau, and Ensigns Haberlin, Denicke, and Count von Rantzau‡ are captured. In the death of the brave Brigadier Fraser, who died from his wounds the day after the battle, the army has sustained

---

* Bernhard Rich. Dahlstirna. He, as well as Captain Fredersdorff, died of his wounds the following year at Albany, so that the writer's kind wish was not gratified.

† Gottlief Joachim Gleissenberg. He died February 20, 1801, as Colonel commanding at Wolfenbüttel.

‡ Ensign Count von Rantzau, Ernest August, was drowned in the Schuylkill while in captivity.

a great loss. Sir Francis Clarke [Clerke], Captain and First Adjutant of General Burgóyne, and who only a few years since studied in Göttingen, is also killed. Major Acland is likewise wounded, and a prisoner. His wife, a born " my lady," who shared his tent with him throughout the entire campaign, is his true and faithful companion in captivity. Both these persons, whose parents are still living, are already in possession of a yearly income of £20,000 sterling. Aide-Major Bloomfield of the artillery, and Captain Green, Brigade-Major of General Phillip's division, are wounded. Furthermore, several other officers have been either killed, wounded, or captured. During the night succeeding the battle we were engaged in taking down our tents and sending back our baggage.

On the 8th of October we danced a minuet backward! and merely showed the enemy our teeth and claws. We did, however, considerable damage with our cannon. In the night we began our retreat, and arrived at Saratoga in the evening. Bad roads and abominable weather caused us to leave in the enemy's hands some baggage and a number of cannon.

On the afternoon of the 10th, General Gates appeared with his army, and stationed himself on the heights near the church at Saratoga.* The Fishkill,

---

* All of the prominent places mentioned in the campaign and retreat have, through the energy of Mrs. E. H. Walworth of Saratoga Springs,—a Trustee of the " Saratoga Monument Association," and whose grandfather was in the battles,— been marked by handsomely inscribed granite tablets, put

which could very comfortably be waded, alone separated the two armies from each other.

On the 11th, the enemy crossed the Fishkill with
several brigades; but my Lord Balcarras opened fire
upon them with his cannon, driving them back with
loss. They, however, captured our bateaux, some
provisions and other articles, together with one English officer and forty men. During the 11th, 12th, and
13th the cannonading never ceased, while the fire of
musketry between the outposts of the two armies was
incessant. The enemy continued, with their superior
numbers, to hem us in, until by the 14th of October
retreat was impossible. Our provisions also had by
this time so diminished that hunger stared us in the
face. Again, not only was the enemy's position a
strong one, but they outnumbered us four to one; so
that, even should we have chanced to defeat them,—
which, by the way, was highly improbable,—our condition, so far as our stomachs were concerned, would
in no wise have been improved. To force them back
upon Albany at one *coup* was not to be thought of.
The enemy, moreover, did not deign to attack us, as
they hoped that in a few days hunger would cause us
to surrender without the shedding of blood. To
abandon our artillery and baggage, and fight our way
with bayonets through the terrible wilderness back to
Carillon, seemed the only thing left for us. But even

---

up by Booth Brothers of New York City, who also built the
Saratoga Monument.

this idea had to be abandoned ; for it had by this time become plain to us all, that without any resources the larger portion of us would die a most miserable death upon the journey. We therefore preferred an honorable capitulation to an ignominious death.* The

---

* Governor Horatio Seymour, in his oration at the laying of the corner-stone of the Saratoga Monument, said : " Monuments not only mark but make the civilization of a people ;" and Lord Macaulay, in his comments on the siege of Londonderry, wrote : " A people which takes no pride in the noble achievements of remote ancestors will never achieve anything worthy to be remembered with pride by remote descendants." The Saratoga Monument, which now in massive granite commemorates the surrender of Burgoyne, practically illustrates these sentiments of those two great men. This monument, which overlooks the Field of the Surrender, is 40 feet square at the base, and 154 feet in height; and as it stands on a bluff 350 feet high, it has an altitude above the river level of 554 feet, thus affording from its summit a magnificent panoramic view of the adjacent country. It is an obelisk, combining the Egyptian and Gothic styles of architecture. The interior of the first two stories is lined with sixteen bronze *alto-relievos* (two-thirds the size of life), illustrating different scenes in the campaign,—such as the murder of Jane McCrea, the burial of General Fraser, and the passage of Lady Acland to the American camp. Three of the exterior niches contain bronze figures in heroic size of Schuyler, Gates, and Morgan ; the fourth one—like the niche of Marino Falieri at Venice—being left vacant with the name of ARNOLD inscribed underneath. Its architect was J. C. Markham of Jersey City, N. J., and its builders, Booth

SARATOGA MONUMENT.

Corner-stone laid October 17, 1877.

(To face page 126.)

enemy met us half-way,* and the 14th, 15th, and 16th of October were passed in negotiating. On the evening of the 16th both generals agreed upon the articles of capitulation, which were thirteen in number, and were as follows : †

On the 17th of October our army marched to the banks of the Hudson,‡ stacked their arms (neither of the enemy's officers nor commissioners being in sight),

---

Bros. of New York City, who with great liberality made no charge for the corner-stone.

The " Saratoga Monument Association," under whose auspices the monument was erected, and whose president is the patriotic and public-spirited Hon. John H. Starin, has lately come into possession of the eight bronze field-pieces captured from Burgoyne at the time of his surrender. To the praiseworthy efforts of the late Hon. S. S. Cox, who introduced in Congress the first bill for these cannon, and also to the energy of Hon. John Sanford, who completed what the death of Mr. Cox left unfinished, is due the fact that these cannon will in a few months grace the base of the monument. Among these cannon are the twelve-pounders captured from our friend, the old "twelve-pounder," Major Williams !

* Or, literally, " The enemy extended to us his hand."

† As these " articles" are to be found in any authoritative history of the United States, and also in my " Life of General Riedesel," they are here omitted.

‡ Within the then plain intrenchments of " Old Fort Hardy "—erected in 1757 under the superintendence of Col. James Montresor, an accomplished military engineer, and named after Governor Hardy, the royal governor of the colony of New York.

and began their march to Boston. The Canadians, and most of the Provincials who had fought on our side, started in boats for Lake George. These latter are from this time forward to be looked upon as exiles. However, it is the intention to send their unfortunate families after them, but without any of their earthly possessions.* We passed the enemy's encampment, in front of which all their regiments, as well as the artillery, were standing under arms. Not a man of them was regularly equipped. Each one had on the clothes which he was accustomed to wear in the field, the tavern, the church, and in everyday life. No fault, however, could be found with their military appearance, for they stood in an erect and a soldierly attitude. All their muskets had bayonets attached to them, and their riflemen had rifles. They remained so perfectly quiet that we were utterly astounded. Not one of them made any attempt to speak to the man at his side ; and all the men who stood in array before us were so slender, fine-looking, and sinewy,

---

* The condition of these Provincials was most unfortunate, particularly as their *status* was left very undefined. The Provincial officers, it was feared, would be treated as prisoners, without any standing as to exchange. Indeed, I have now before me a *MS.* letter from General Fraser, given to one of these Provincials previous to the Battle of Saratoga, designed to protect him in case of capture. See also General I. Watts de Peyster on this subject. General de Peyster's works have an authoritative value ; and his writings, as well as those of General Rogers, cannot be too highly valued by the historical student.

that it was a pleasure to look at them. Nor could we but wonder that Dame Nature had created such a handsome race ! As to their height, dear brother, the men averaged from 6 to 7 inches, according to Prussian measurement ; and I assure you I am not telling an untruth when I state that men 8 to 10 inches high were oftener to be seen than those of only 5 ;* and men of larger height were to be found in all the companies. Captain ——, who was chagrined at not having succeeded in obtaining recruits among these people, will corroborate me in this statement. I am perfectly serious when I state that the men of English America are far ahead of those in the greater portion of Europe both as respects their beauty and stature. In regard to the gentler sex, I will give you some details of them also when I arrive at Kinderhook ; and now for a space devoted to American wigs ! †

Few of the officers in General Gates' army wore uniforms, and those that were worn were evidently of home manufacture and of all colors. For example,

---

* That is, 5 feet, 8, 10 and 5 inches. In the Prussian army a man must measure at least 5 feet to be accepted as a soldier. So that when an officer, or for that matter, any German, speaks of the height of another as being " 8 or 10 inches," he means that he stands 5 feet 8 or 10 inches. These 5 feet are never mentioned in speaking of his height, as that is an understood thing.

† The writer evidently makes a pun—the persons whom he goes on to describe being contemptuously known as " *Whigs*," and some of them, as will be seen further on, wearing *wigs*, which he proceeds humorously to describe.

brown coats with sea-green facings, white linings, and silver dragons, and gray coats with yellow buttons and straw facings, were to be seen in plenty. The brigadiers and generals had, however, uniforms to distinguish them from the rest of the officers, and wore a band around the waist to designate their respective rank. On the other hand, most of the colonels and other officers wore their every-day clothes. They carried their muskets (to which a bayonette was attached) in their hands; their pouches or powder-horns were slung over their backs, and their left hand hung down by their side, while the right foot was slightly put forward. In one place could be seen men with white wigs, from beneath which long and thick hair escaped—thick lambs' tails hanging down from the back; in another, the glistening black wig of an abbé surmounting some red and copper-colored face; while in still another, white and gray clerical-looking wigs made of horse and goat hair, and piled up in successive rolls. In looking at a man thus adorned one would imagine that he had an entire sheep under his hat, with its tail dangling around his neck. A great deal of respect is entertained for these wigs, not only because they are supposed to give the wearer a learned appearance, but because they are worn by all the gentlemen composing the committees and those who are renowned for wisdom. The gentlemen who wear these different kind of wigs are mostly between fifty and sixty years of age ; and having but recently begun to wear them, you can imagine what a comical appearance they cut as soldiers. The determination which caused them to grasp a musket and powder-horn can be seen in their faces, as well as the fact that they are not to be fooled with, especially in skirmishes in the woods. Seriously speaking, 'this entire nation has great natural military talent. There were many regiments of regulars [Continentals] in the enemy's army who had not been properly equipped, owing to the lack of time and scarcity of cloth. They have flags with all kinds of emblems and mottoes.

It must also be said to the credit of the enemy's regiments, that not a man among them ridiculed or insulted us; and none of them evinced the least sign of hate or malicious joy as we marched by. On the contrary, it seemed rather as though they desired to do us honor. As we filed by the tent of General Gates, he invited the brigadiers and commanders of our regiments to enter, and when they had done so he placed all kinds of refreshments before them.

Gates is a man between fifty and sixty years of age ; wears his thin gray haii combed around his head ; is still lively* and friendly, and constantly wears spectacles on account of his weak eyes. At head-quarters we met many officers, who showed us all manner of attentions. Philadelphia officers, men of our own blood, offered to make our stay in Pennsylvania among their loved relations pleasant and agreeable. French officers overwhelmed us with a thousand complimentary

---

* This word in the original may also be translated *jovial.*

speeches; apd a number of officers formerly in the Prussian service were fairly in ecstasies at the sight of our blue coats—bringing back to them recollections of the battles of Sovr [Sohr], Prague, and Kesselsdorf. Brigadier Weissenfels of Königsberg has rendered many services to those of our officers (seven in number) who were taken prisoners [at the battles of Saratoga].* We marched to-day to *Freeman's Farm*, four English miles distant.

---

* Weissenfels, Frederick H., Baron de, born in Prussia in 1738; died in New Orleans, La., May 14, 1806. During his early life he was an officer both in the Prussian and the British service; but emigrating₁ to this country, he settled in 1763 in Dutchess Co., N. Y. He became Lieutenant-Colonel of the 3d N. Y. battalion in 1776, and afterward commanded the 2d N. Y. battalion at White Plains, Trenton, the battles of Saratoga, and the battle of Monmouth. He accompanied Sullivan's expedition against the Six Nations in 1779, and fought at Newton. The war left him impoverished; and at the time of his death he filled a minor office at New Orleans. He was honored by a military funeral, in recognition of his services at White Plains, Trenton, the battles of Saratoga, Monmouth, and Sullivan's expedition. One of his daughters' descendants is Mr. E. Ellery Anderson, a lawyer in New York City. He was also one of the original founders of the Society of the Cincinnati; and his fellow Germans deserve to be chronicled here in appreciation of their share in the great work of securing the independence of the American Republic. One of these, and his associate in founding the Cincinnati, was Sebastian Bauman,—who, by the way, has not had the recognition which he deserves,

December 15, 1777.

FRIENDS : You will now have to march 215 English miles (about 45 German) in order to be with me in

---

and therefore we give for the benefit of future historians a sketch of his life.

Sebastian Bauman was born at Frankfort-on-the-Main, Germany, April 6, 1739, and was educated as a military engineer at Heidelberg University. He emigrated to this country when quite young, and settled in New York as a merchant. He served through the Revolution as major in Colonel Lamb's regiment of artillery, being commissioned by the New York Provincial Congress early in 1776. At the evacuation of New York by the Americans, on September 15, 1776, he was the last officer to leave the city. He was left in the morning with orders to bring off what artillery remained ; but being cut off from the rest of the army by the extension of the British lines across the island, after the landing at Kipp's Bay, he waited until nightfall, when he succeeded in transporting his guns—two howitzers—and men to Paulus Hook. He also served in the northern campaigns of 1776 and 1777, and was in command of the artillery at West Point, from 1779 to 1781. In 1781 he took part in the siege of Yorktown, and at the close of that campaign returned to West Point, where he remained until the close of the war. In 1782 he published, from his own surveys, the only American map of the siege of Yorktown. He took part in the entry of the American army into New York on November 23, 1783, being in command of the artillery, viz., two companies of the second (Colonel Lamb's) regiment. When the army was disbanded he returned to New York and resumed his old mercantile pursuits, taking, however, command of the New York regiment of artillery in the State service. In October, 1789, he was appointed postmaster of the critical situation in which we at present find ourselves upon Winter Hill.

On the 8th of October we marched to Stillwater—three and a half English miles from where we were when I last left off [i.e., Freeman's Farm]. The old ruined fort * at this place, as well as the vicinity within

---

New York, which position he held until his death, October 19, 1803, the anniversary of the surrender of Cornwallis. A great-great-grandson, Bauman L. Belden, now (1891) resides at Elizabeth, N. J.

The statement of the writer, that so many French and Prussian officers were in General Gates' army, is quite a new revelation. There were doubtless, however, numbers of foreigners fighting on the side of the colonists, whose names have not come down to us.

* At Stillwater, in June, 1709, Colonel Peter Schuyler, in command of the advanced guard of General Nicholson's army, halted and built a small stockaded fort, which he called Fort Ingoldsby, in honor of Lieutenant-Governor Major Richard Ingoldsby. Again, in the summer of 1756, General Winslow, while on his Northern Expedition, halted at Stillwater, and, building a new fort on the decaying remains of the old one erected in 1709, called it Fort Winslow. —*N. B. Sylvester's History of Saratoga Co.* It is to this fort that the writer refers.

In September, 1777, General Gates, in passing up the Hudson on his way to Bemus Heights, first made his stand at this old military station at Stillwater. After remaining here, however, for a day or two, he, probably with the advice of Kosciusko,—for Gates, himself, was seemingly incapable of any original ideas save those of intrigue,—changed his plan, and going up the river about a mile further, threw up his memorable intrenchments on Bemus Heights.

a radius of three miles, derives its name from the gently flowing river [Hudson], which here has the appearance of a quiet inland lake. The English corps crossed the Hudson in order to take a certain route for Boston.* Here we obtained fresh provisions, and our palates, which had by this time become accustomed to salt provisions, recovered their normal tone by means of the fresh meat.

On the 19th we crossed the Hudson in a few boats, and as night had by this time overtaken us, we could not go any further towards Shetekok [Scaghticoke], a hamlet composed of Dutchmen—a rich and highly interesting people. Accordingly, we were obliged to bivouac here in a meadow placed at our disposal. From this time on we began to find great abundance of apples, from which an incredible quantity of cider is made both in New York and all the New England States, and which can be kept from three to four years. At this place they first began to steal our horses—an infernal proceeding, which they have kept up through our entire march. By way of comfort they tell us that we have either stolen them ourselves, or else have

---

* The Germans went to Boston by the route outlined by the writer ; but the British went by the old " Hoosac Road " by way of Northampton—the same by which John Norton and the captives of Fort Massachusetts went in the opposite direction to Canada. In other words, over the old Indian road over the Hoosac to Deerfield and Northampton. —*Letter from Prof. A. L. Perry, of Williamstown, to the Translator.*

bought them from persons friendly to the king, who in turn have stolen the horses from them! Moreover, they further tell us that we will now become acquainted with the old Roman law, *Ubi rem meam invenio, ibi vindico.* We cannot understand, however, how they can confound Canadian and German horses with theirs!

On the 20th of October, we passed many Dutch and German farm-houses. The farmers have immense stores of grain, large heaps of which lie in mows covered with movable roofs. We went this day as far as New City,* a small town on the Hudson, but lately started, being only eight years old. It was originally founded by two individuals named French, who have built beautiful dwellings and ware-houses. Both of these gentlemen, however, being Tories,—that is, friendly to the king,—they were forced to abandon their property. Bakers, smiths, and artisans had established themselves in this village, but most of the houses were standing empty. We found here a well-equipped hospital, in which we met several wounded soldiers belonging to our army. They told us that they were given tea, sugar, chocolate, and wine, notwithstanding these articles were extremely dear.† Our troops had to bivouac at this place and encounter the discomforts of a snow- and rain-storm during the night. Our march to-day covered ten miles.

---

* The present town of Lansingburg, N. Y.

† This treatment was in marked contrast with that which our prisoners received from the British in New York and the South.

On the 21st, it rained and snowed during the entire night. The houses were a quarter of an English mile and even more apart, and the roads were hilly and bad. After covering fourteen miles, we arrived at Greenbush, and put up houses [of boughs ?] in a wood near the dwelling of a rich farmer named Woolesworth. During the night it froze hard.

On the 22d, our march was almost entirely through woods, in which every little while we came across miserable dwellings. Finally, after going twelve miles we came to a plain lying between several hills, where the borough of Kinderhook (consisting of about seventy straggling houses) is situated. The most prominent house in the village belonged to a man named Van Schaaken [Van Schaak].* It was built of stone, and three stories high. This man showed us many little attentions, and was a kind friend to us. The rest of the people, who were Dutch by birth, were also kind. They had but one fault—that is, they were selfish, and were as fond of money as a Jew. Every article they sold us was terribly dear. Most of the houses were very well built, and nicely finished inside. The inhabitants in general lived well. Their breakfast consisted of milk, tea, roast-meat, baked apples, and all kinds of rich butter-cakes. We could have made ourselves comfortable enough with tea, if we had only had enough of it. Those people who were in comparatively easy circum-

---

* Van Schaak was a Tory or Neutral, and was very cruelly treated afterward.

stances had gilt frames around their mirrors, and very good pendulum clocks. Similar household furniture can be found all along the road to Boston. As all the barns of the farmers were full of grain, we had to camp out in a neighboring wood.

December 18, 1777.

FRIENDS : I am at last in Kenderhook [Kinderhook], whence I promised to write you a chapter about pretty girls. Before, however, reading my narrative to a lady, examine it carefully so as to see if there is any danger of its causing future trouble between me and my dear countrywomen. Should you decide against it, have mercy on me, and upset the ink-stand on the entire chapter !

The ladies in this vicinity, and as far as Boston and New York, are slender, of erect carriage, and, without being strong, are plump. They have small and pretty feet, good hands and arms, a very white skin, and a healthy color in the face which requires no further embellishment. I have seen few disfigured by pock-marks, for inoculation against smallpox has been in vogue here for many years.* They have, also, exceedingly

---

* This remark seems to us, at the present day, singular ; but not so when it is remembered how bitterly both the clerical and the medical professions fought against inoculation—the former, indeed, inveighing against the practice from the pulpit—and when it is also recalled that the deaths in London alone from smallpox fell during the last century but a trifle short of 200,000. Indeed, so common was it, that Macaulay says that "a person without a pitted face was the exception."

white teeth, pretty lips, and sparkling, laughing eyes. In connection with these charms they have a natural bearing, essentially unrestrained, with open, frank countenances, and much native assurance. They are great admirers of cleanliness, and keep themselves well shod. They frizz their hair every day, and gather it up on the back of the head into a *chignon*, at the same time puffing it up in front. They generally walk about with their heads uncovered ; and sometimes, but not often, wear some light fabric on their hair. Now and then some country nymph has her hair flowing down behind her, braiding it with a piece of ribbon. Should they go out (even though they be living in a hut), they throw a silk wrap about themselves and put on gloves. They have a charming way of wearing this wrap by means of which they manage to show a portion of a small white elbow. They also put on some well-made and stylish little sun-bonnet, from beneath which their roguish eyes have a most fascinating way of meeting yours. In the English colonies the beauties have fallen in love with red silk or woollen wraps. Dressed in this manner, a girl will walk, run, or dance about you, and bid you a friendly good-morning or give you a saucy answer according to what you may have said to her. At all the places through which we passed dozens of girls were met with on the road, who either laughed at us mockingly, or now and then roguishly offered us an apple, accompanied by a little courtesy. At first we thought they were girls from the city, or at least from the middle classes ; but lo and behold !

they were the daughters of poor farmers. Notwithstanding the many pretty things I have said about the
gentler sex in this country, I must still give my loved
countrywomen the credit of possessing certain gentle,
lovable, and languishing qualities which lend additional
attractions to their charms, but which are entirely
lacking in the beauties to be found here. Most perfectly formed and beautiful nymphs are to be seen on
all sides ; but to find one endowed with all the attractions of one of the graces is a very difficult thing.*
Enough of this, however. I think it high time to bring
this disquisition to a close ; and I shall now do so after
stating that the fair sex were the cause of our losing
some of our comrades on the 23d of October.†

---

* This was probably said to neutralize among his countrywomen when he should return to his fatherland, the encomiums
he had lavished upon the American women. Perhaps, however, the recipient of this letter, acting on the writer's hint,
threw the ink-stand over this portion !

† That is, by desertions. In fact. both all along the line of
this trip to Cambridge and during the stay of the Germans in
Pennsylvania and Virginia, many deserted, and taking American wives, founded families who are among the most respect-
able of our citizens. In going through Berkshire Co., Mass.,
particularly, the Yankee girls had most seductive charms for
the German captives. Johann Hintersass (John Henderson)
"stayed over at Williamstown, and founded a family who are
now still in existence."—*Prof. A. L. Perry of Williamstown
to the Translator.* Indeed, says Rosengarten in his " German
Soldier in the Wars of the United States," " of thirty thousand Germans who were in the Revolutionary War, hardly

To-day being a day of rest, I shall give you an account of two things which particularly struck me in this country. The first of these was the evident mastery that the women possessed over the men. In Canada this power is used by the women to further the interests of the men ; but here it is used nearly to ruin them. The wives and daughters of these people spend more than their incomes upon finery. The man must fish up the last penny he has in his pocket. The funniest part of it is, that the women do not seem to steal it from them ; neither do they obtain it by cajol-

---

half returned, and the large portion of those who remained did so voluntarily, making their new home the beginning of a new life very unlike that of their native land." Mr. Rosengarten also tells us that the late General Geo. A. Custer, who lost his life in a battle with the Sioux Indians, was a great-grandson of a Hessian officer who served under Burgoyne. After the latter's surrender he was paroled, settled in Pennsylvania, married there, changed his German name, " Küster," to one easier to pronounce in English, and moved to Maryland, where the father of General Custer was born in 1806. I quote, as also in point, the following extract which I copy from the *General Advertiser and Morning Intelligence* of 1777 : " If America has been the grave of a great number of Germans, some of them, however, have found it the road to fortune ; and among the latter we learn is Colonel De Mengen, who, having been taken a prisoner of war, had the good fortune to become acquainted with Miss Hancock, only daughter of the late President of the American Congress, and obtained the hand of that rich heiress, who is besides endowed with the most amiable qualities, and with whom that fortunate officer has gone to settle in Philadelphia."

ery, fighting, or falling into a faint. How they obtain it—as obtain it they do—Heaven only knows ;
but that the men are heavily taxed for their extravagance is certain. The daughters keep up their stylish
dressing because the mothers desire it. Should the
mother die, her last words are to the effect that the
daughter must retain control of the father's money-bags.
Nearly all articles necessary for the adornment of the
female sex are at present either very scarce or dear,
and for this reason they are now wearing their Sunday
finery. Should this begin to show signs of wear I
am afraid that the husband and father will be compelled to make their peace with the Crown if they
would keep their women-folks supplied with gewgaws!

The second thing which attracted my attention was
the negroes. From this place to Springfield few farm-
houses are met with that do not have one negro family
living near by in an out-house. Negroes, in common
with other cattle, are very prolific here. The young
are well fed, especially at the calf age. Take it all in
all, slavery is not so bad. The negro is looked upon
in the light of a servant to the farmer, the negress doing all the heavy housework, while the pickaninnies
wait upon their young white masters. The negro is
sometimes sent to war instead of his youthful owner ;
and for this reason there is scarcely a regiment in
which you shall not find some well-built and hardy
fellows. Many families of free negroes are also met
with here who reside in good houses, are in comfortable circumstances, and live as well as their white

neighbors. It is an amusing sight to see a young negress—her woolly hair gathered up in a knot behind, a
sun-bonnet perched upon her head, and encircled by a
wrap—ambling along, with a negro slave shuffling in
her wake.

On the 24th we marched through Cleverac [Clav-
erack], a small hamlet inhabited entirely by Frenchmen. The pastor of the place stood in the road with
several of his flock, and bestowed upon us his apos-
tolic benediction. We ascertained that from being a
stocking-weaver he had developed into a servant of
the church.* Thus is it in America, and, alack! almost entirely throughout the Evangelical Church. It
is but a short time since that a former sergeant-major
in the Prussian army, who had become the pastor
primarius of the Evangelical church at Albany, created a great sensation. Meeting two of his congregation in a tavern, who remonstrated with him for treat-
ing his young wife too harshly, he clubbed them so
severely that one of them died from the effects of a
broken head, and the other had both of his arms shat-
tered. Since that time he has been wandering from
place to place a fugitive, and at present is acting as
pilot on a ship. This piece of news was told me by
Mr. Tielemann, our marching commissary, who is a
native of Manheim, and a member of the committee

---

* This practice was common at one time in Germany. An
edict of the year 1557 forbids all incompetent artisans from
entering the priesthood for the purpose of gaining a livelihood.—*Note by Schlözer.*

in Albany, major of a militia regiment, proprietor of a tavern in that city, and by profession a shoemaker. The English churches have regularly ordained ministers, and the Dutch churches have their ministers direct from Holland.*

We marched 17 miles to the wretched village of Nobletown, where we were forced to encamp in the open air on account of a scarcity of houses. The night became so frosty that in the morning we looked like sugar-coated toy-men.

On the 25th, after passing over miserable stony and rocky roads, that led partly through woods, we arrived at Great Barrington, where we took up our quarters, having marched 13 miles. A rougher and more spiteful people I never saw. Our patience was often stretched to its highest tension on account of our churlish treatment. Most of our officers were not allowed to cross their thresholds, but, in common with their soldiers, had to take up their quarters in filthy stables and barns. This place has a fine and well-built church.

On the 26th we passed through Tyringham, and across forests and veritable wildernesses. At first we swore at the abominable roads, but ceased when we found they became worse, as cursing could not do them

---

* In fact, up to 1820, the Dutch Reformed Church at Paulus Hook (Jersey City) received all its ministers from Holland; and up to 1825, the morning service was conducted in Dutch, and the afternoon in English.

justice.* Presently we entered a large and wild moun-
tainous district, called Greenwood †—dismal enough
to silence the most disobedient child by threatening to
send it there if it did not behave itself. After marching 17 miles we encamped in this American Caucasus ;
while, to make things still more uncomfortable for
us, it rained the entire night.

On the 27th of October it rained still more ; and the
roads became so horrible that a curse was merely a
waste of breath. At length, after marching 11 miles
we took up our cantonments in twenty different
houses, situated about three good English miles from
Blandford. In these houses seven regiments and our
escort of 700 men were quartered. To-day I felt so
vexed and taciturn that I threw myself upon an
open barn-floor, hoping to get some rest ; but the cold,
together with a wind- and hail-storm that was raging,
banished all sleep. Then, again, the thoughts of to-
morrow's march stung me more even than the fleas,
which seemed to be holding a "general congress"
around my body.

On the 28th we had alternately hail, rain, and snow.

---

* This reminds one of the story of the extremely profane
New England wagoner, who, perceiving the loss of his load
after ascending a high hill, sat down making no remark. To
a passer-by who, knowing the man, said, " Why don't you
swear?" he replied—in the very same words of the writer—
" I can't do it justice !"

† Greenfield is here meant—a town in Franklin County
Mass., on the west bank of the Connecticut River.

The wind was so piercing, that, no matter how warmly we wrapped ourselves in our cloaks, it penetrated to the very marrow. In addition, our wet clothes froze as stiff as iron. A grenadier froze to death upon the march, many pack-horses were lost in the same way, and since that time I am firmly convinced that a man can endure a greater amount of hardship than a horse. The oldest soldiers admitted that they had never before experienced such a march. Towards evening, we had advanced only ten miles to Westfield, a very neat little village. The experience that we had passed through that day so aroused the sympathies of the inhabitants, that they opened their doors to us. It is the custom in this place to put lightning-rods on the churches and all the handsome buildings and houses, to prevent their being struck by lightning. From here, and even as far as Boston, you shall find this invention of the learned Franklin in universal use, both in the cities and the country. I have never seen anywhere larger cattle and swine. A certain author, whose name I do not now recall, did not lie when he wrote that along the Connecticut River oxen weighing 1800 and hogs 500 pounds (English weight) were to be met with.

On the 29th, the rain continued, accompanied 'by snow and hail. The roads were still bad, but not so dreadful as before. After covering 7 miles we arrived at West Springfield, a village of scattered houses, with its own church. The Connecticut River divides this town from East Springfield. We were taken into the

houses of the villagers. The people were tolerably
kind, but damned inquisitive. From this village, and
in fact from the entire neighborhood, whole families
of women and their daughters came to visit us, going
from house to house to gaze upon the prisoners.
From the general down to the common soldier, all had
to stand inspection. The higher the rank of the person so visited, the longer they stayed and "sized him
up"! I was delighted when they soon left me, but
my brigadier, in spite of his horrible grimaces, was not
so fortunate. I offered chairs to the pretty girls, and
by this means gained time partially to revenge myself
by staring at them in my turn. Finally, we became
tired of this sort of thing, as one party after another
continued to enter our rooms without knocking. I
actually believe that our host charged an admission-fee
to see us.

On the 30th, we had a day of rest. Early in the
morning I had myself shaved, and powdered my hair.
It is the custom of the women and girls in this neighborhood either to sit upon side-saddles or ride upon
pillows placed at the backs of their husbands or gal-
lants. Very often a young beauty may be seen leading an entire caravan [cavalcade?] at full gallop. The
young "bucks," with their miserable clothing and female trappings, look as if they had stolen their attire
from the women themselves.

On the 31st of October we started out, intending
to cross the Connecticut River—a feat which we were
not permitted to perform ; for, notwithstanding our

entreaties, the regiments were relegated into a wood
3½ miles distant, by the Committee of East Springfield.   East Springfield is an exceedingly lively little
village, with very pretty houses.   It is true that they
lie from 50 to 100 paces apart, but this space is either
a yard or a garden, which is separated from the street
by a fence.   The gardens also contain statues.   This
place is a veritable magazine for the storage of weap-
ons for the Americans; and it has also a small but very
well-built armory or arsenal.   We here saw various
parks of artillery with their trains, and, among other
things, twelve entirely new 4-pounders of French
make.   The store- or magazine-houses were filled from
top to bottom; and workmen of all trades were seen
in all the houses engaged in the manufacture of am-
munition-wagons, guns, etc.   I have seen here wagons
which could not have been better made in England,
and upon which the " R. P." was painted as neatly as
the " G. R." *   Order prevailed everywhere; and an
old man with a wig and a large gray overcoat attracted
my special attention by his scolding and the noise that
he made.   I ascertained that he was Master-General of
Ordnance; and at that moment I wished that my old
friend —— had been here to see his colleague, look at
his dress, and observe the energy he displayed.

---

* General De Peyster, on excellent authority, informs me
that these letters stand for " Reserved Park " and " General
or Grand Reserve"—" Park" in the latter case being understood.   " Grand Park " in connection with artillery is a well-
known technical term, as well as " Reserve Park."

On the 1st of November we marched to Palmer—a miserable hamlet some 12 miles distant, where from necessity we were obliged to encamp. From this place as far as Boston mile-stones are set up at the distance of every mile.

On the 2d, our march led through West-town (a village containing good houses and wealthy inhabitants) to Brockfield [Brookfield], 15 miles further. The people of this village refused to admit us into their houses, claiming that neither General Gates nor Colonel Reid,* who commands our escort, could demand it of them.

On the 3d, we passed through Spencer and Luster or Leicester, the people of which villages were in the same mind as those of Brockfield, and treated us in a similar manner.

On the 4th, a short march brought us to Worcester —a thriving little city. After much discussion the citizens finally allowed us to occupy their houses and barns—the battalion of Bärner being quartered in a large meeting-house. Our brigadier and myself lodged with a lady of distinction who had two sons in Howe's army, and whose husband was residing for the time being in England. She was obliged to pay rent for living in her own beautiful house, and her furniture had been levied on by the Committee. In order, also,

---

* General George Reid, colonel of the N. H. Second at the battles of Saratoga. In 1785 he was a brigadier-general of militia, and in 1791 sheriff of Rockingham County, N. H. He died September, 1815.

to make her life as happy and tranquil as possible, the Committee had taken possession of her land, and in fact exercised a general supervision over her entire possessions! To prevent, moreover, anything from being stolen, the Committee have put large locks on the house. This lady, whose condition we pitied from the bottom of our hearts, received us with attention and friendliness. She had been well brought up; and her two very handsome daughters seemed to pattern after her. Indeed, we hesitated to receive the many attentions she showered upon us, and insisted upon doing our own cooking. The elder daughter presented her betrothed to us—a very worthy young man, who in his turn introduced us to other reputable young men in the town. These in former days had servants to wait upon them, but were now compelled to bow the knee before the gentlemen composing the Committee. In every city, village, and county Congress has appointed Committees, who rule subject to its approval, and see to it that all of its decrees are obeyed. Indomitable zeal in the maintenance of liberty and the execution of the commands of Congress, are the necessary requisites for membership in this Committee —a membership which confers upon one the power to rule over his fellow-citizens. These gentlemen were in other times plebeians; and Heaven help him who is suspected by them of being a Tory! Many families are now living under this suspicion. At their command the minister leaves the altar, and the male members of his congregation grasp the musket and the powder-horn.

In this town we received 15 thalers of paper-money (or about 90 shillings in the same currency) for one guinea; although, according to a law passed by Congress, one guinea is supposed to be worth in paper-money 28 shillings. Since then we have paid the Americans in their own coin, who otherwise would long ago have pulled the wool over our eyes, since six shillings in paper is supposed to be equal to five shillings in silver. All articles of food and drink are five and six times dearer than formerly; and all on account of this paper currency, for which the public have no liking, but which is issued in enormous quantities by Congress and all the provinces. Hence all goods have been raised to a high price to meet the corresponding [depreciated] value of this paper-money; for otherwise the merchants would suffer great loss. The fact that, up to the present time, coin can so readily and advantageously be exchanged for paper-money is, it is said, to be ascribed to the Tories. In part this is true; for many Tories have exchanged their paper-money for coin, so that in case of their being persecuted by party spirit they can easily leave the country with ready cash.* It is not true, however, that the

---

* The idea of the writer is not very clear, though his language has been rendered, as usual, literally. I presume he means that the Tories having taken away most of the coin that was in circulation, the Americans were very glad to exchange their paper for the gold and silver of which they stood in want.

Tories have done this either through hatred of the Americans or a liking for us. Every one in this country thinks too much of his own precious self. Even the most zealous republican tries to get rid of his paper-money, and thinks more of one guinea than they do of $15 in paper-money, which is supposed to be equal in value to 15 piasters. Furthermore, merchants who buy their goods from Frenchmen and Hollanders have to pay for them in coin, for the reason that American paper is not current in Europe. This makes gold very scarce and high; and consequently, the merchants raise the price of goods to such an extent, that they not only receive the cost of the goods in return, but a tremendously big profit besides. There have been times when 17 thalers have been given for one guinea. On some occasions people come from different points with tons of this paper-money, which they desire to exchange. It is true that Congress is very watchful with regard to this paper currency, and keeps a sharp eye on the smugglers. The penalty has been fixed at large sums of money, and also imprisonment; but there are so many ways of evading this, that it is almost impossible to catch them at it. Just at present the French and Hollanders will take paper-money in return for these goods, but they soon come back and exchange it for our specie.

I will now give you several examples showing the high prices ruling here. A tolerably decent hat, which I was compelled to buy, cost me 25 rixthalers. A yard of cloth, which costs $2\frac{1}{2}$ rix-thalers at home, cost 2½ guineas here. Four shirts, that I was obliged to buy, cost me 4 guineas. At home a yard of linen can be bought for 5 *groschen.* The necessaries of life are also pretty high. The wine is dear and bad, and a bottle cannot be bought for less than 20 *groschen* of our money. The paper on which this letter is written (seven sheets) cost 18 shillings (paper-money), or more than 1 rix-thaler of our money.

On the 5th of November, we tramped through Shrewsbury and Northborough to Marlborough, 16 miles further.

On the 6th, our way led us to Sudbury, a hamlet in which we found a train of artillery, a magazine, and other implements of war. We camped in West-town 13 miles distant. At last, on the 7th, we passed the village of Watertown, marched through Cambridge, and entered the barracks of " Winter-Hill," where we are now living in misery.

A "hill" is called in German a *hügel;* and the entire neighborhood between Cambridge and Boston is filled with a number of equally bare and treeless hills, which, for the most part, are covered with barracks. " Winter-Hill," and " Prospect-Hill," which adjoin it, have so many barracks that on one the Germans are quartered, and on the other the English. The barracks are without foundations, and built of boards, through which the rain and snow penetrate from all sides. They contain merely dormer-windows; and our people have to endure a great deal of hardship while in them, as they afford not the least protection against the cold. Batches of four and five officers lie in holes in which it is impossible to turn one's self. Wood is so sparingly dealt out that there is not enough to keep the fire burning on the hearth. Within a distance of 5 English miles no trees or bushes are to be found ; and for this reason wood is very dear.

Generals Burgoyne and Phillips had no quarters assigned them, and were, accordingly, forced to take up their abode in a tavern. Major-General von Riedesel and his staff were quartered in some wretched houses in the vicinity of the Hills. Afterwards, all the generals were assigned to good houses in Cambridge : the brigadiers, however, were obliged to remain in their miserable quarters. My brigadier and myself are living in a house ; our room is on the ground-floor ; and the cracks in the walls are so large that you can see everything going on outside. I never felt so cold before in my life. Indeed, I did not dare to leave the hearth ; and the ink on my pen was frozen more than a hundred times. If we had a snow-storm, accompanied by wind, the snow would be a foot deep in my room. The poor soldiers in the barracks had to endure still greater hardships ; for they had neither straw nor any covering whatever.

At the foot of Winter-Hill lies the village of Mystic, which is separated from the village of Millford [Medford] by a small river. Both villages contain good houses and numerous artisans. Boston, a much larger city than Brunswick [in the duchy of Brunswick], is but four English miles distant, and presents, with its harbor and ships, a fine appearance. None of us, from the highest to the lowest, is allowed to enter it under penalty of being sent to the prison-ships.* The wife of General von Riedesel on various occasions had permission from the Governor to drive into the city to visit some ladies. Between Prospect-Hill and Boston lies Bunker's Hill, upon which General Gage's fortifications may yet be seen. It is covered with barracks. Beneath this hill lies Charlestown, which was burned down by the above-named general in his retreat. Several handsome houses have already been erected on it.

Cambridge is a small place, having no attractions save Harvard College and its large buildings. The College church has an antique Roman appearance. The houses in the vicinity of Cambridge are quite grand, and give the neighborhood a look of importance. Many of them are the country residences of the rich merchants of Boston. In Cambridge a regiment of Provincials, together with a train of artillery, lie quartered in barracks for the protection of the town. There is also a large magazine here.

On a hill near Prospect-Hill a regiment of Americans are stationed. They have drawn a chain of outposts about the hills on which we are quartered, and through which no subaltern or soldier is allowed to pass without a permit from General Heath, Governor

---

* So it seems that the Americans had prison-ships as well as the British!

of Boston. For disobeying this order the offender is liable to be shot. Two English soldiers have already been shot by the sentinels, and forty English soldiers, who were arrested without passes by the patrol, have been sent to the prison-ships. As yet we have had no such experience in our corps. A great deal of animosity exists between the American and English soldiers; and a number of encounters that have taken place between them have made our stay here still more irksome and unbearable. At first no officer could ride or walk farther than a mile. This has now been changed to a three-mile limit. These boundaries are patrolled by sentinels; and an officer would risk a great deal if he overstepped these bounds. The staff-officers have also quarters assigned to them now. Many have refused to leave, but have caused their barracks to be placed in better order.

General Burgoyne as well as Major-General von Riedesel gave a ball, to which they invited a number of ladies from Boston and its vicinity. The Committee, however, issued the most stringent orders forbidding any one to attend; and consequently the invited guests, with two notable exceptions, failed to put in an appearance.* These were the two daughters of General Schuyler, one of whom is married to a Mr. Carter,† both of whom dared to disobey the order. It

---

* A very small piece of business on the part of General Heath.

† This was Angelica, the eldest daughter of General Schuyler, a beautiful and brilliant girl, who married an Eng-

was General Schuyler himself who furnished Major-General Riedesel with the addresses of his two daughters, and the Committee therefore said nothing about it. We have no intercourse with anybody excepting ourselves. Large *fêtes* are not given ; and Generals Burgoyne and Phillips live in a very retired manner. As we live far apart from each other,—for instance, General Riedesel is about a mile and a half away from us,—and as the roads in winter are in a wretched condition, most of us live a solitary kind of life. The German and American officers hold no intercourse with each other. The regiments [American] stationed here are made up of militia, ahd are mostly working-men. We had great trouble in convincing the inhabitants that our officers had no civil profession ; and even when they were convinced of that fact, they labored under the idea that it was because our officers were too capricious to work.

December 30, 1777.

President Hancock has now been several weeks in Boston. His arrival was welcomed by the ringing of bells and the firing of cannons. This man, whom

---

lishman, John Carter Church. He came to this country under the name of Carter, having fled from England on account of a duel. He was a man of large wealth and good social standing, and on his return to England he resumed his name of Church, and entered Parliament. His son, Philip Church, owned a beautiful seat about three miles from the village of Angelica, N. Y., which he so named in honor of his mother.

the most zealous republicans call "the American king" in order to provoke us, looks, to all appearance, worthy of the position he holds as the first man in America. Moreover, he is so frank and condescending to the lowest, that one would think he was talking to his brother or a relative. He visits the coffee-houses of Boston, where are also congregated the poorest of the inhabitants—men who get their living by bringing wood and vegetables to the city. Indeed, he who desires to advance in popularity must understand the art of making himself popular. In no country does wealth and birth count for so little as in this; and yet any one can maintain the position given him by fate without being in the least familiar with the lowest.

Those of our officers who are really captives are to be found partly in Westminster and partly in Rutland;* but those of our subalterns and privates who are prisoners are scattered far and wide. In one sense of the word the captive officers have more liberty than we, for they are at liberty to go wherever they please, provided they have permission from the commissioners in charge. Many of them have received leave to go to Canada, and not a few have visited us, remaining four weeks and even longer. They were, however, obliged to pay for everything they bought in specie, as they had had no opportunity of exchanging it for paper currency. Moreover, they have to pay

* In Worcester County, Mass.,—not Vermont.

two and three times as much for the necessaries of life at the places where they are stationed than if they were in Boston. The profit made by the merchants of this country on their goods is almost beyond belief. If I buy any at fourth hand I can rest assured that I am paying sixteen times as much as I would otherwise have paid had I bought at first hand. Some articles would even be still dearer than they are if it were not for so many French ships arriving here. One pound of St. Omer [tea] can be bought of them for $1\frac{1}{2}$ silver piaster, or 2 thaler in our money; while the merchants in Boston would not sell it for less than $2\frac{1}{2}$ piasters. The French pay us daily visits on the hills for the purpose of disposing of their wares. They also furnish us with our reading. They sell us comedies and tragedies in single numbers, which they have brought along to wile away the time on the voyage over.

The captured privates were at first confined on the prison-ships; afterwards they were allowed to go into the cities and the country and earn a living for themselves. Many of them were compelled by necessity to do this, and people from places 80 and even 100 English miles distant come to Boston to hire them. Those having trades get along nicely, and are, besides, able to earn money. Those that have no trades are obliged to thresh, chop wood, and do other menial offices. All sergeants, aye, and even some of the ensign standard-bearers, have to work and attend upon the farmers. The food they receive is good, and they are not forbidden to tap the cider-barrel. Each inhabitant who has a prisoner must be responsible for him. He can, however, discharge him, provided they let those in authority know of it. Time alone can tell whether some of these young and unmarried chaps will not be captured by the daughters of the people for whom they are working.*

January 1, 1778.

MY DEAR FRIENDS : I wish you a right happy New Year, and expect soon to have the pleasure of hearing from you.

January 5th : To-day we received the sad news that the worthy and upright Captain von Dahlsijerna had died at Albany on the 23d of December. Here also, in the barracks, Lieutenant Pflüger, a brother-in-law of Colonel Baum, has just died of consumption. By way of comfort, on the other hand, we have received greeting from Major Lutterlob, formerly in the Brunswick service, but now Quartermaster-General in Washington's army. Major von Mengen also received a visit from his cousin, a doctor of medicine named Schmidt. He, Mengen, is in excellent circumstances, and is married to a very near relative of President Hancock.†

January 13th : Our *ennui* increases and becomes almost unbearable. Very often the weather prevents

---

* This proved in very many instances to be the case, especially in Virginia and Pennsylvania. See preceding note.

† A daughter. See note *ante.*

us from going out for a walk or a ride. The Canadian winter is golden in comparison with this ; for
while there we never had such continuous penetrating
and cold winds. Up to the present time the winter
has been one continuous storm. The winds are so
violent that they cause our wooden houses to rattle
and tremble. In connection with this, the weather is
variable. One day we have a thaw, and on the next
the cold is as intense as in Canada. We have had an
astonishing amount of snow, and yet only four days of
good sleighing. Sleighing here, both as regards the
roads and horses, cannot be compared with that in
Canada.

The chief amusement we have at present is a suit
between General Burgoyne and an American colonel
named Hanley [Henley]. The former accused the
latter of attempting to kill an English soldier upon
Winter-Hill. The case is being tried by an American
court-martial made up of two colonels, two lieutenant-colonels, two majors, and four captains, with Brigadier-General Glover presiding. The mode of con-
ducting these trials is different from ours. The
court-house is an oval building, having on all sides
large church windows reaching to the roof. The inside is nothing but a large hall, the middle of which is
partitioned off by a railing and two steps leading to a
platform, thus making one half of the room one foot
and a half higher than the other. At the further end
and opposite the large door the President sits upon a
chair, which, when he stands up, nearly reaches to his

breast. On each side of this chair the assessors sit, those of higher rank occupying more elevated seats than those of lower. All, however, have a wooden casing—something like a desk—before them. In front of the President's chair a large square table is placed at which sits the *Advocatus Causæ*,* with the plaintiff on his left hand and the defendant on his right, while they in turn have their counsellors or assistants at their side. The counsellors of General Burgoyne are Generals Phillips and Von Riedesel. Each party has four or five officers sitting on the opposite side of the table, who, as well as the Judge Advocate, take notes of the proceedings. The Judge Advocate examines the witnesses; and the President and assessors, aye, even the plaintiff and defendant, are also allowed to question them. These questions, together with their answers, are put down in the minutes. On these trials long speeches are made by either side, having reference to the bearing of the law upon the matters under consideration. In several instances General Burgoyne demonstrated his abilities as a great orator, and caused the entire court to shed tears. The trial grows daily more and more protracted; and it would seem as if the attack made upon the soldier by Colonel Henley (who, by the bye, has charge of all the magazines) was caused by a dispute between him and the English soldiers while the

---

* That is, the Judge Advocate-General—in this instance Lieutenant-Colonel Tudor.

provisions were distributing. Henley's main defence appears to be an attempt to gloss the matter over by ascribing his act to zeal in the performance of his duty. In all probability the minutes of the proceedings will be printed. Every male person is allowed to attend these trials and to take notes thereof. The court-house is jammed; for even the humblest person is allowed to attend.*

---

* For the merits of this case—though not for its details, which are nowhere described so graphically or so fully as in the text—the reader is referred to General Heath's Memoirs. As this work is extremely rare, and therefore not easily accessible, it may be stated that Colonel Henley's offence was, in the words of General Heath, as follows: " Another serious matter took place about this time : Colonel Henley, who had the immediate command at Cambridge, a brave and good officer, but warm and quick in his natural temper, having ordered some prisoners who were under guard turned out that he might examine them, one of them treated him, as he judged, with much insolence, upon which he pricked him with a sword or bayonet. General Burgoyne immediately presented a complaint against Colonel Henley, charging him with barbarous and wanton conduct, and intentional murder." General Riedesel's account is materially different, and is in these words: " On the 8th of January the American Colonel Henley, with his men, was on guard behind the barracks on Prospect Hill. In front of one of the barracks stood eight English soldiers belonging to the 9th Regiment. They were engaged in conversation, when suddenly the above-mentioned colonel ran in among them with a drawn dagger like a maniac, and in an instant mortally wounded two of the group." A sharp correspondence fol-

Jan. 30*th :* Up to the present time no one has been allowed to go into Boston, though, since we have had permission to go to Charlestown (which is sepa-

---

lowed between Heath and Burgoyne, which resulted in a court-martial, the result of which was an acquittal in these words: "The court, after mature consideration, are of opinion that the charge against Colonel Henley is not supported, and that he be discharged from his arrest. The general approves the opinion of the court, thanks them for their unwearied endeavors to investigate the truth, and orders Colonel Henley to assume his command at Cambridge immediately. The general thinks it to be his duty on this occasion to observe, that although the conduct of Lieutenant-General Burgoyne (as prosecutor against Colonel Henley) in the course of the foregoing trial, in his several speeches and pleas, may be warranted by some like precedents in British court-martial, yet as it is altogether novel in the proceedings of any general court-martial in the army of the United States of America, whose rules and articles of war direct that the Judge Advocate-General shall prosecute in the name of the United States, and as a different practice tends to render courts-martial both tedious and expensive, he does protest against this instance being drawn into precedent in future." The writer in the text, it will be noted, speaks also of the long-drawn-out trial. Colonel David Henley died January 1st, 1823, at Washington, D. C., and was at the time of his death a clerk in the War Department. He was an officer of merit, and during his career held various important positions in the United States Government. Col. David Henley has sometimes been confused by historians with his brother ,Maj. Thos. Henley—also on Gen. Heath's staff—who was killed in the skirmish at Montresor's Island (now Randall's) in Sept., 1776.

rated from Boston by a small bay), I have been enabled to see the latter city from a short distance. This, however, has only whetted my curiosity to see its interior. The ringing of the city's bells is very fine, Boston, also, is famous for its chimes.

Feb. 5, 1778 : To-day has been one of the happiest I have experienced since I came here. Commissioner Messero, who has general charge of all the prisoners, has brought a large bag full of letters from Boston. It is true that they have all been opened and read, but this does not matter. The letters were forwarded from Rhode-Island to Boston, and it is said that there are still more at the former place. I received eight letters in all, the oldest being dated on the 4th of March, 1777, and the most recent on the 3d of September. I cannot convey to my friends the pleasure I experienced on receiving so many letters, and in their own handwriting too ! Commissioner Messero, a Dutchman by birth, has been—take it all in all— exceedingly friendly to us. But when shall this letter be so fortunate as to be read by you ?

Our situation is daily becoming worse. Differences, disputes, misunderstandings, and quarrels seem to be the order of the day.* The Americans are beginning

---

* In this connection it may be well to quote from the Narrative of General Riedesel two occurrences similar to that of Colonel Henley, having a far more tragical ending, which took place in Cambridge some months later. The quotation is made for the purpose of showing that our adversaries in the Revolution suffered nearly as many grievances at our

openly to accuse us of breaking the articles of capitulation, and are unfairly trying to saddle the blame

---

hands as we experienced from theirs. It is to be feared that the brutal Cunninghams, of unsavory New York Sugarhouse memory, were not confined to the British side. Here is the account: " On the 14th of June a new difficulty arose between the Provincials and a Brunswick soldier of the regiment Rhetz, which cost the latter his life. He was on the point of going beyond the chain with his young and beautiful wife, who had followed him from Europe, when six brutal militiamen began joking with the woman in a coarse manner. The husband in protecting the honor of his wife finally found himself forced to defend her and himself with a cane against their assailants. The sentinel near by witnessed the unequal combat with all composure, but when the German drove back the Americans, he ran up and thrust his bayonet through him. The poor man soon expired. Riedesel again complained bitterly to Heath, whereupon the latter sent the murderer to Boston for trial, but it could never be ascertained what was done to him. . . . A still sadder case, however, occurred a few days later, on the 17th of June. On that day the English Lieutenant Broune, with two Boston ladies, rode down Prospect-Hill in a one-horse carriage. [The English occupied Prospect-Hill and the Germans Winter-Hill.] The road was very steep, and the horse consequently was going at full speed. At the foot of the hill a double guard of Americans was stationed, whose duty it was to watch that portion of the road lying outside the chain, and also the storehouse at this place. The guard, although they must have known Broune by his uniform, nevertheless called to him to stop. This it was impossible for him to do at once, as the horse was running at full speed. He therefore turned round to show his sabre,

upon us.* This much is certain, viz., that General
Gates, it is said, intends to throw up his command

---

thereby indicating that he was an officer. Notwithstanding
this, however, the Americans ran up with fixed bayonets;
and one of them, regardless of the ladies in the carriage,
fired a bullet through the head of the officer. He died a
few hours afterwards. General Phillips, upon hearing of this
circumstance, was fairly beside himself with anger, and during his first excitement wrote a note to General Heath which
resulted in his being placed under arrest. This occurrence
caused a general excitement in both camps, especially in
that of the English. Some officers who had hastened to
the scene carried their mortally wounded comrade into the
camp, and caused his murderer to be arrested. The latter
was also sent to Boston, but nothing was heard of his being
punished. According to rumor, the fellow was sent to the
army of General Washington, where, perhaps, other oppor-
tunities were given him of showing his bravery in a similar
manner to an unarmed foe. On the 19th the deceased was
buried with all military honors, from the church at Cambridge, Heath having given his consent to it. In the *cortège*
were several American officers of high rank."

* This is a question which has given rise to a vast amount of
discussion, and regarding which much has been written upon
both sides. It is certain that one of the articles—viz.: No.
VI., specifying that " nothing belonging to the king should
be hidden"—was violated, Mrs. General Riedesel, by her
own account, having secretly packed away the German
colors in her private baggage and carried them home—a
feat which she seemed to consider (see her letters) a most
praiseworthy act! The colors of the 9th English regiment,
also, concealed by Colonel Hill at the Surrender, in violation
of the same article, are now (1891), as my friend Mr. J. J.

and refer the matter to Congress. In many respects it would be a sad thing for us all should we have to remain here for any length of time longer; though, on the other hand, should we be sent into the interior of the country we would be widely separated, besides having to pay for the necessaries of life four times as much as we do here. No life can be more unhappy than an idle one, and knowing, as we do, that our present state of idleness is an enforced one, we pass our lives as if in sleep. We have no means of occupying our time, neither have we books with which to wile away the weary hours.

Feb. 15*th:* The suit against Colonel Henley is still on, and the proceedings are carried over from day to day. We can obtain no reliable information from the vicinity, and I have made up my mind to believe nothing that I hear. The number of lies that are printed * and carried from mouth to mouth is almost beyond belief. In reference to matters in Canada we are still in the dark. The Americans are talking about a large expedition of three corps that is said to

---

Dalgleish of Edinburgh, Scotland, informs me, in the Military Chapel at Sandhurst, England, and have been photographed. However, for a most thorough and exhaustive discussion of this entire matter the reader is referred to *Hadden's Journal,* most ably edited by Gen. Horatio Rogers of Providence, R. I., and published by Munsell & Sons of Albany, N. Y.

* It would seem that the newspapers of that day were not so very different from our own!

have been sent to that province, but for many reasons we do not believe it. General Howe has his head-quarters in Philadelphia, and Congress is now sitting at York-Town. Many recruits are being drummed up by the Americans and drilled into shape.

March 1st: The suit against Colonel Henley has finally come to an end, and, as might have been expected, has ended to his advantage. The colonel has been acquitted, all of his conduct being ascribed to his zeal. We have had such penetrating cold that the strongest fire on our hearth has been insufficient to keep us warm.

March 18th: To-day an officer sent by General Burgoyne to Congress returned with the news that Burgoyne will be allowed to return to England for a time for the benefit of his health. But, alas! it has been almost decided that we, or rather the entire army, shall be detained in this country, and that Congress shall not be bound by the articles of capitulation. What will now become of us? We have, however, a little comfort in hoping that our letters may now perhaps be forwarded to our loved friends, but the permission we have received to bring our baggage from Canada, and also the other articles sent to us there from Lower Saxony, hardly consoles us. The soldiers have already worn their clothes for three years, and that, too, on ship-board, through woods, and during the winter in the barracks! The officers, who on leaving Canada took nothing with them except their worst clothes and those that they were then wearing,

are now sighing for new apparel.   Nor do we expect
their   arrival   before   July.   Meanwhile   no one   can
foretell what may happen.   I will send unsealed letters to my dear friends ; but it is little they will contain beyond the fact that I am still living and in good
health.   For the time being, the letters we send to
Canada are also required to be unsealed.

March 27*th :* My letter is still lying upon the
table, and who can tell when it will be sent ?   The
departure of General Burgoyne may be put off for
some time yet ; and it is still doubtful whether my
letter can be sent sealed.   If this privilege is denied
me, it shall remain here.

April 2*d :* Unexpectedly, I have received word
that General Burgoyne intends to depart to-morrow.*
For this reason I am obliged to close my letter without any further additions, excepting to send my best
regards to my dearly loved friends.

June 12*th :* This letter has been lying sealed up to
date, on a board placed over my hearth, because no
sealed letters were allowed to be sent away.   Captain
O'Connel† intends to start for Europe ; but whether

---

* Burgoyne arrived at Newport, by way of Boston, the
7th of April, 1778, and sailed for England from that port on
the 14th of the same month.

† "Captain Laurentius O'Connel [Riedesel's adjutant]
asked permission of Riedesel to return to Europe and arrange some pressing family affairs.   As the presence of this
brave officer could now be of little use, Riedesel did all in
his power to further his wishes.   In the middle of June he

he will be able to take my letter with him or not, I do not know. I earnestly hope that he may.

---

received permission from Congress to return to Europe on parole. Riedesel took this opportunity to send by him his dispatches to his court ; also the flags which he had saved. [See note *ante.*] These flags the captain left in Rhode Island. They were afterward carried to Canada by Lieutenant-Colonel Specht."—*Stone's translation of the Military Journals of Major-General Riedesel.* Captain O'Connel died in 1819, as a pensioned lieutenant-colonel, in Ireland.

LETTER FROM A GERMAN OFFICER, IN THE BARRACKS NEAR BOSTON, FEBRUARY 5TH, 1778.

An American frigate named *Boston* will leave here next week to carry back to France thirty-one French officers who have been serving in the Provincial army. I have become acquainted with many of these gentlemen, who on their departure have offered me their services to communicate with my relatives and friends. I have therefore the pleasure of giving you some news by way of France, as it is difficult to send you letters by any other route.

I am well, notwithstanding our last misfortune [Burgoyne's defeat], and a devouring desire to return to Europe. But not daring to write you anything which would put you *au fait* with my reasons for desiring to leave America, I may say, that for all my reasons I refer you to a letter which I have confided to our M——, who has left us for Canada. It went last December, and perhaps by this time it is in your hands.

Our destination appears very uncertain, and God knows whether we will leave America this year or not.

I doubt it, as it is rumored that we are to be sent into the country among the inhabitants. Regarding which plan, as things go, your compatriots, who are prisoners, greatly complain.

We live in barracks upon a mountain [Winter-Hill] two leagues from Boston. They are built of boards, and the windows are of paper, so that we have had plenty of fresh air this winter. Each barrack is occupied by 4 officers, or 20 soldiers. If our furniture were better, and our dress and equipments, now so ragged as scarcely to cover our nakedness, would only hold out, it would not be quite so bad.

The dearness of all articles in this part of the world is awful, and surpasses the imagination. We pay for a hat 52 florins, while a pound of tea costs 32 florins; a shirt, not remarkably fine, 3 guineas; a pair of woollen stockings, 10 florins; and as to woollen cloth, it cannot even be obtained. You may judge from all this of the situation of a subaltern who has for his support only his pay.

Fifteen days since, a packet of letters for the German troops arrived at Boston. Overflowing with joy, I expected to receive some lines from either my relatives or friends in Europe. Judge, then, of my surprise when we were told that the packet had been opened in the town; that only eight letters had been forwarded to our chief, and that the remainder (some 500 letters) were in the hands of the citizens, who were passing them from hand to hand!

LETTER FROM A BRUNSWICK OFFICER.

CAMBRIDGE, NEAR BOSTON, IN NEW ENGLAND.

Oct. 10, 1778.

Heaven be praised that we now have an opportunity of sending off some letters! We still sit here in our cage, anxiously waiting for the hour of our deliverance. Speaking in American official language, we yet bear the title of "Conventionists," but in reality we are only *prisoners*. Still, our hopes continue to be fixed upon Sir Henry Clinton, who, we trust, will effect our exchange. Nature, it is true, has spared nothing to make this country in every way pleasant and delightful; but in our present circumstances we heartily wish that we were again wandering in the wilderness through which we came to this place. Even the attractions of the pretty girls who are to be found here in large numbers, and who, being entirely neutral in reference to the war, ardently maintain the *jus naturæ*, cannot overcome our longing to leave our present quarters.

To correspond safely has become more and more difficult, and therefore you need not expect any more letters from me. The prison-ships, with which the refractory are threatened, are even now lying before our very eyes.

Some seven weeks ago the French fleet arrived in Boston, and since then 9000 more troops are said to have arrived—a circumstance which has caused everything to be outrageously dear. Neither have we yet received our baggage. To clothe an officer from fifty to sixty guineas are required, according to present prices. You can picture to yourself, therefore, how we are going about! Nevertheless we are still elegantly "frizzed" and "gotten up," because we have abundance of time to devote to our personal adornment. The flour which is used for our bread—or, as we call it, *poudre royale*—is not spared on our wigs. The French officers are polite enough to pay us occasional visits; only we, however, do not dare to return the compliment. How my fingers fairly itch to write you of some of the contrasts here presented,[*] if I only dared to do so. The French and Americans do not at all like each other, and the former often express themselves to us about it in no very light terms. Of Canada we know nothing. The English regiments have been removed into barracks at Rutland,[†] which the first of us who were prisoners named Siberia.

Several days since I received letters actually dated

---

[*] That is, I suppose, between the French and the Americans.

[†] Rutland in Massachusetts, near Worcester—not in Vermont.

a year ago, and were old enough to have teeth! They have given me no end of pleasure.

FROM THE SAME.

Nov. 13, 1778.

I send with this an accurate drawing of a bird's-eye view of Boston and of different Canadian places, sketches of Indians, etc. If the rebels had not captured before the capitulation my secretary (who, by the way, is now serving on the rebel side as a captain), with all my sketches and drawings of the campaign of 1777, I should have been able to send you more.*

On the 25th of last month our General von Riedesel received orders from General Heath, the commandant at Boston, to put the German troops in readiness to march. The English regiments, which for several weeks past have been quartered at Rutland, fifty-three English miles from us, have already set out for Virginia in three divisions. Our first division, which consists of those of the dragoons who survived the affair at Bennington, Mengen's grenadier battalion, and the regiment of Rhetz, left on the 9th of this month; the second division of Riedesel's and Specht's regiments

---

* I suppose that many of the officers, generally skilled draughtsmen and of much intelligence, made quantities of sketches illustrative of the scenes through which they passed. What a treat it would be if we possessed them! Lieut. Aubury—attached to the Army of Burgoyne—did something in this direction.

on the 10th ; and the third will be made up of the survivors of Bärner's battalion, the Hesse-Hanau regiment, and the Hesse-Hanau artillery.

Our destination is Albemarle in Virginia, distant
from here 583 English miles, or 120 German. Should
I have the opportunity, you may reckon on receiving
from me more detailed accounts of our prospects, the
nature of the country, etc. It is a sorry thing for us,
and especially for the privates, that our baggage, which
has lately arrived at Newport, is to be brought by sea
to Philadelphia, and will not reach us until we arrive
in Virginia. We will therefore have to make our
weary and painful march in rags and tatters ; and will
receive our clothing and equipments in a climate
where, on account of the heat, we shall have but little
use for them.

LETTER FROM STAUNTON, VIRGINIA.

STAUNTON, IN VIRGINIA, JUNE 1, 1779.*

The departure of Captain Edmonstone,† former aide-de-camp of General von Riedesel, again furnishes me with the longed-for opportunity of sending you proof that I am still living. Have you yet received the letters I wrote you in February of this year from Charlottesville, and in April from here,‡ in the former of which I described our woful wanderings during the winter from Boston to the county of Albemarle in Virginia, and which lasted from the 10th of last November until the 16th of January of the present year? At least, I consigned them to the protecting care of all the patron-saints of Great Britain, that they might be insured, not only against the attacks of Neptune and his mighty vassals, but against all Christian flags, pirates, and American privateers!

---

* This letter arrived in Brunswick Nov. 10, 1779.—*Note by Schlözer.*

† A young Englishman who studied at the Collegio Carolino, in Brunswick, shortly before the outbreak of the American Revolution.—*Note by Schlözer.*

‡ They did not arrive.—*Note by Schlözer.*

178

Would to Heaven that I could at last read the con-firmation of my hopes regarding your own welfare, as well as that of our friends and dearly-loved relatives. Your letters of September, 1777, are as yet the last we have received from our Fatherland; * and this mournful uncertainty only increases our longings to hear from you.

We still find ourselves in the same awfully disa-greeable position, and the hopes that we have at times entertained have so often came to naught, that we hardly dare venture to hope that we have finally done with our inactivity, confinement, vain wishes, and many other vexations. It is true, that since my last letter our baggage, which we have looked for so long and anxiously, has at length arrived from Canada; but even this pleasure has been a vain one to not a few of us. In my trunk, for instance, I have found nothing excepting articles in a state of utter decay, and from the appearance of which it is difficult to say what they might have been at some former time. I regret, especially, one of my chests in which I had packed the furs I had bought in Canada, and which is now said to have been burned in the service of the king. In fact, I have saved nothing except what I brought with me from Saratogha.† Indeed, if only our mount-

---

* Since this date numerous letters have been sent from Brunswick to the corps, and, therefore, could not have arrived. —*Note by Schlözer.*

† The Indian spelling of Saratoga.

ings [uniforms], and especially our linen wear, which we ordered from Brunswick in the spring of 1777, had arrived, we might have consoled ourselves for our other losses. Now, however, on account of the incredible dearness of these articles, we are obliged to submit to paying fifteen times more for them than we have been used to paying even for the actual necessaries of life. Our remittances of money, moreover, come slowly ; and although we negotiate occasionally some paper-money, we have to suffer a loss at least 40 per cent. We were happy in Boston—far happier however, in Canada. We are living here in such an out-of-the-way nook of Virginia—yes, I might say, separated from the rest of the world—that we neither hear nor see anything new, nor receive anything new in the way of reading-matter. We learn of nothing going on in our vicinity, much less of anything from remote quarters. A few days since an English corps undertook to make a landing at Hampton, threatened Williamsburg, and caused a feeling of disgust* throughout the entire province, and consequently among us.

The heat here is intense ; however, the sultry air is almost daily cooled off by thunder-storms as terrible as can possibly be imagined. Towards the end of February the peach and cherry trees had already blossomed ; but towards the middle and end of April

---

* The idea of the writer probably is that they were all chagrined that the English were not successful in their attempt.

all the fruit became frozen—even the rye and winter wheat suffering severely.*

Of good neighbors we have none, because hardly a gentleman can be found within a distance of forty-two miles of Staunton. Real gentlemen, however, can be met with nearer to the coast, who are very rich and jovial, and own well-furnished houses of fourteen rooms or more. These exercise hospitality in the noblest manner, often keeping a stranger with them for three weeks.

Since my last, written from Charlotteville, we have marched forty English miles further to Staunton, the capital city of Augusta County. On our journey I passed the famous Blue Mountains, and as a consequence have approached nearer the Ohio and Mississippi. Staunton has about thirty houses, of which twenty-four are built in the same style as the very common ones in Zellerfelde.

The barracks are about thirty-four English miles from here, and this circumstance often affords me the opportunity of giving myself very healthy exercise, not to speak of taking off my hat in these strolls through the woods to large thick snakes—who, however, are quite polite as long as my horse does not step on them. Our barracks, of which I gave you a sketch in my previous letter, and which must have

---

* This only shows, as I have said in another note, that all the talk of so-called weather experts is mere twaddle! The seasons are about the same, year after year.

caused you to commiserate me, may be compared with those in the city of Ninroch in their best days.*

The English soldiers have built covered walks in front of their barracks, and all of their streets resemble the Brunswick Yungfernstiege.† The Germans, on the other hand, being lovers of vegetables, have laid out and planted countless gardens; and in order to raise poultry, they have started poultry-yards, which they have surrounded by palisades. These German gardens are a great attraction for visitors from even sixty or more miles away; and a cock, which ordinarily could be bought for one shilling, will now bring half a guinea should he show fighting qualities. Many officers who formerly lived at quite a distance have had barracks built near the soldiers, which well merit the name of good houses.

The 21st English regiment have built for their use a large church. Church-yards, wells, in fact every-

---

* Other letters arriving at the same time with this letter describe these barracks as being thin partitions of wood, in which the soldiers either ran the risk of freezing or of being burned at their fires and suffocated with the smoke. The march to reach them is described as terrible, because night quarters for them had either to be obtained by force, or else they had to encamp during the night upon snow four to five feet deep in the woods.—*Note by Schlözer.*

† Literally, "Maiden's Hill," in the same way as Maiden Lane, New York City, was called by the Dutch "Maiden's Valley." At the time the writer wrote, the "Yungfernstiege" was a fashionable promenade, having on its top the armory of the City of Brunswick.

thing which can be made, are in good condition. Two American speculators have lately built taverns, which already contain two billiard-tables. A company of English soldiers have likewise erected a comedy theatre, in which two performances are held weekly, and in which three sets of scenery have already been put up. On the drop-curtain a harlequin is painted, with his wooden sabre pointing to the words, " Who would have expected all this here ?" The *parquette* costs four and the *parterre* two paper dollars. The officers lend the necessary clothing to the actors ; and drummers are transformed, for the nonce, into queens and belles ! Some very fair plays are acted, which, on account of their satirical nature, do not always please the Americans ; and on this account, that their ears may not be offended, they do not visit these comedies.

You may believe that all of this is literally true. The soldier desires to show that he can laugh at everything, and, in himself, can find means to make life endurable and comfortable.

A large number of houses and sheds have been built by the soldiers, as they found, on first coming here, that the barracks were absolutely unendurable from their terribly bad condition. As it is, the men are greatly confined, and it is even now proposed to encircle their already limited area by palisades. Provisions have alternately been passably good or shockingly bad ; and extras are either not to be had at all, or are obtained only at incredibly high prices.

Heartily, yea, yearningly, do we hope that ultimately we will be free once more. Those officers of our corps who were captured in the engagements [battles of Saratoga], and, being intended for exchange, had already arrived in Rhode Island, were obliged to return to Massachusetts-Bay, the exchange being discontinued.

We thus live as much scattered about in North America as the Jews are throughout the entire world— of which nation, by the way, very few are to be seen, either here or in any part of America. In fact, you may travel one hundred miles without meeting with a single family of that nation.

In conclusion, I wish I could put into this letter a pipeful of genuine Virginia tobacco, which is here smoked without being prepared, and for that reason is uncommonly strong.

Only remain a friend to myself and my ——, and have the kindness to deliver the enclosed letters.*

---

* The captives at Saratogha are therefore enacting a roll in Virginia similar to the one played by the captives in Poltawa in Russia and in Siberia, sixty years ago.—*Note by Schlözer.*

LETTER FROM A HESSIAN CHAPLAIN.

BROOKLAND, NEAR NEW YORK, Sept. 7, 1776.

I have put up some posts in the ground and laid a board on it for a desk, upon which I will write and tell my dearly loved brother that upon the other half of our globe I am in health, happy, and grateful to God. I also walk out every pleasant morning and admire the beautiful clouds which ascend from the valleys to the heavens overhead.

Notwithstanding I have seen such solemn and majestic scenery upon the ocean, I am inexpressibly glad to set foot on Staten Island. Scarcely can I restrain myself from kissing God's earth. Is she not our mother?

Our loved Hessians assimilate themselves to their surroundings in all things; and I remember them in my sermons, and in my prayers during the still hours of the night, while on my bed, that they may be strong in Christian courage. The delay of the English generals makes them impatient, while the offensive look cast upon the Germans by the English excites still more their ire. This state of feeling caused lately a bloody affray. A subordinate officer of the Yägers, to whom an Englishman said while drinking, "God damn you Frenchmen, you take our pay," answered calmly, " I am a German, and you are a S——."* Thereupon, both of them whipped out their swords, and the Englishman received such a gash that he died of his wounds. The brave German was not only pardoned by the English general, but the latter issued an order that the English should treat the Germans like brothers. This will be done the more readily as the intelligent German has already begun to speak a little English.

Our first movement forwards was an attack against the rebels,† who defended themselves more poorly than one would have expected from persons who had the stimulus of a love of freedom. The slaughter was horrible, more especially by the English troops, upon whose ranks the Germans drove the rebels like sheep.

---

* The animosity between the Germans and French was well known, so that the English soldier mentioned in the text probably used the epithet " Frenchman" designedly as a term of reproach. Duponceau, one of Baron Steuben's aides, writing of his journey with that general, says: " I remember that at Manheim the Baron, with a significant look, pointed out to me, at the tavern where we dined, a paltry engraving hung up on the wall representing a Prussian knocking down a Frenchman in great style. Underneath was the following appropriate motto : ' Ein Franzman zum Preuszen wie eine Mücke. A Frenchman to a Prussian is no more than a musquito'! "

† The Battle of Long Island, fought Aug. 27, 1776. This shows also that the Americans did more execution upon the enemy than the latter would have us believe.

O friend! it was to me a terrible sight when, the other day, I went over the battle-field among the dead, who mostly had been hacked and shot all to pieces. Many of these were Germans, which gave me the greater agony. We have taken many prisoners, who would mostly have taken service with us had they not been prevented by the English.

The Indians, many of whom are in our vicinity, are not like those which Rosseau and Iselin have described. On the contrary, they are all very obliging, friendly, and used to work, supple as the deer of the forest, and not without a belief in God. When I hold up my right hand towards heaven, they fold their hands upon their breasts and bow themselves low to the ground.

DESCRIPTION OF NEW YORK, LONG, AND STATEN ISLANDS, IN 1776.

NEW YORK ISLAND, IN THE TERRITORY OF HARLEM, 5 ENGLISH MILES FROM THE CITY OF NEW YORK, AND 100 YARDS FROM HORNHUCK* ON THE EAST RIVER.

Sept. 18, 1776.†

DEAR FRIEND :

It was, in truth, easy for me to promise to write you a letter from America when I last parted from you in Göttingen ; but really up to now it has been very difficult for me to fulfil my promise. Indeed, I would not have even yet been able to fulfil it had I not been living for several weeks as an invalid—a situation nevertheless, if I must say it, very agreeable to me, being in a most delightful part of the world, and

---

* Now " Harris Hook" (from Eighty-ninth to Ninety-first Street, New York). This hook was known in the Revolution as " Horn's Hook," and previously as " Horen's Hook." A strong redoubt called Thompson's Battery was erected on this Hook, which commanded the mouth of Harlem River and the narrow channel at Hell-gate.

† From the late Lieutenant Hinrich to the Editor.—*Note by Schlözer.*

free from all the turmoils of war and its alarms. I
fulfilled my promise to ———, on whose account, as you
know, I became a soldier. Here, then, for a few jot-
tings down of the adventures through which I have
passed, though I could not possibly have room to tell
you all that I have lived through and encountered.

Last Sunday (the 15th of September) we landed,
amid the loud cannonading of five sloops-of-war, in
flat-boats from Long-Island, on New-York Island,
about four miles from New-York City. As riflemen,
we were detailed as an advance-guard; and during
the afternoon we took entire possession of this part of
the Island. Hardly, however, had we taken up our
quarters when a new alarm on the part of the rebels
obliged us to turn out. I had the right wing of the
advanced guard; and as our march led us towards
King's-Bridge, I was most of the time near the East
River, along whose banks are the most beautiful
houses. I had the honor of taking possession of these
handsome dwellings, and also of the enemy's battery,
where I found five cannon. The rebels fled in every
direction. All of these houses were filled with furniture and other valuable articles lawful prizes of war;
but the owners had fled, leaving all their slaves behind.
In a day or two after, however, one head of the family
after another appeared; and tears of joy and thank-
fulness rolled down the cheeks of these once happy
people when, to their great surprise, they found their
houses, fruits, animals, and furniture intact, and learned
from me that I had only taken possession of them for

their protection.   Nor could they believe me until I had turned their property over to them.

A day or two since, the rebels, 4000 strong, attacked our pickets; and we had to endure a heavy fire until afternoon, when I heard that they had been repulsed.   I say "heard;" for at one o'clock I was forced to leave the field, having been shot through the left side of my breast by a rifle ball, four fingers' width from the heart.*   To whose care could I more safely trust myself than those very people who called me yesterday their benefactor and savior, and who received me in the most friendly manner and with open arms ?   As I had never liked noise, and now much less than ever, instead of choosing a palatial residence, as I could have done, I selected a little house on the East River, in which the widow of a preacher, Ogilby,†

---

* For the details of this engagement, known as the battle of Harlem, the reader is referred both to Mrs. Lamb's and to my " History of New York City."   The British stretched from " Horn's Hook" (where this letter is dated) to " Mc-Gowan's Pass," and across the beautiful hills to the northwest, their left flank resting on the Hudson.

† The Rev. John Ogilvie here mentioned was the pastor for many years of St. George's Chapel, built by Trinity Church, on the corner of Cliff and Beekman Streets, New York City, and which some years since gave way to the march of improvement.   His death is thus described in my " History of New York City:" " One of the melancholy events associated with this old church [St. George's Chapel] was the sudden death of Rev. John Ogilvie, who, on the 18th of November, 1774,

from New York had taken up her abode, together with a large number of children and grandchildren. Not far from here was the house—or rather the palace—of her old father, who had managed to retain a large store of porcelain, wine and brandy. All these people returned last evening ; and the sensation I experienced when I saw mother and children, and grand-father and grand-children, etc., and even the black children of the slaves, hugging and kissing each other, excited me to such an extent that my wound threw me into a fever during the night. The amount of flattery that these good people bestowed upon me—which I did not deserve, as I was only obeying orders—cannot be imagined. Oh ! how much I could tell you of this happy country ; but I see that my paper is already half full, and I have not as yet told you how I came to this land, nor what experiences I have met with since I saw you last.

My narrative naturally divides itself into two parts, viz., my experiences upon water and land.

1st. From Bremerlehe, by way of Portsmouth and Halifax, to Staten Island.

Of our life and deeds, the truth and the lies all mingled together, you have doubtless read in all the newspapers. I will therefore pass over everything, confining myself to the Hamburg correspondents. I now take my journal in hand, and as soon as I meet with

while delivering one of his Friday-evening lectures, was suddenly stricken with apoplexy."

anything in it which I think will prove of interest to you, I will jot it down ; so do not lose a night's sleep in bothering over its chronology and synchronisms.

The sea is never green, and in the Bay of Biscay is not black, as several officers have lately described it. On the contrary, it is the color of the sky.

The air on the fishing-banks of Newfoundland is so cold, that although it was in the middle of June, I almost froze in a fur-coat. This is caused by a fog, year in and year out, which covers the banks and the entire coasts of North America to a distance of 15 German miles from the land.

The sea has different degrees of saltness. On the sand-banks it is less salty than in the deep sea, while on the coast of Scotland it is still less so. The nearer it is to the equator the less salty it is.

On the fishing-banks I saw French ships sailing hither and thither, and regarded them with pity. Just look at the former French possessions in this part of the globe on a map of North America for the year 1755, and then compare them with what now remains to them on Danville's map of North America : two islands, Miquelon and St. Pierre, the sole remainder of their former conquests, and neither of which is able to support more than two hundred inhabitants.

Halifax is a wretched city. The streets are mere sandy roads, lined on either side with rows of barracks, and inhabited by shoemakers, brewers (who brew the beer from the bark of trees, and which is very good*),

---

* Spruce beer.

and people of that class. The churches are each of them merely a house about twenty or more paces long, and the arsenal and Government-House are only passable. Poverty, crude art, and scarcity of culture and refinement are to be seen everywhere; houses built only of a few boards, and of exceedingly rude and primitive appearance, stand in a meadow. Horned cattle were scarce and very small; and the few that were to be seen were without herders. The forts and batteries were simply composed of freshly thrown up mounds of sods. Many New-Englanders have come here from Boston, and this influx may probably help develop the province.

Upon anchoring at Sandy Hook, I took a sketch of the vicinity, taking in its harbor, with the result, that I found that all the charts designated the east-south-easterly point of Staten Island incorrectly. They draw the point in the shape of an obtuse angle, whereas it projects so prominently that when you enter close by Sandy Hook you are obliged to sail in a somewhat southerly, then in a northerly, and then in a westerly direction before you can see the *ravelin*. I have rectified this error on my chart.

On the 12th of August, we entered the harbor of New York, or Sandy-Hook, and cast anchor off Hendrick's Point. All that could be seen in the harbor was a fleet of 450 sail, and also a number of boats which patrolled the enemy's coasts, both to guard against our fleet being set on fire and to intercept deserters. Just imagine to yourself one of the finest of harbors, in which 1000 ships can ride, and also fancy the actual number of vessels all crowded with human beings, and surrounded at the same time with a vigilant enemy! Think also of our enjoying the finest of weather; and all of these troops, bound upon a mission on the success of which depends the welfare not only of England, but of this powerful and proud country; and, again, remember that we are engaged upon an undertaking on which the eyes of the whole world are now fixed. So much regarding my sea-voyage.

Now in regard to my stay on Staten, Long, and New York Islands.

Staten-Island is a hilly country, covered with beautiful forests composed mostly of a kind of fir-tree, the odor of which can be inhaled at a distance of two miles from land. The island itself, however, is but sparsely settled. The soil is fruitful. Peaches, chestnuts, apples, pears, grapes, and various kinds of nuts grow here in wild profusion, mingled with roses and blackberry bushes. The climate and soil are, without exception, the loveliest, healthiest, and most agreeable on the face of the globe; and a person, were he so disposed, could easily lay here the foundations of a great fortune for his progeny should he invest a reasonable sum in land. Just about this time everything is still in an uncivilized and poverty-stricken state, for the foraging parties of the rebels and the different encampments of his Majesty's troops have stripped the country of all the necessary articles of life. The so called " Old and New-Town" consists of two houses scarcely 25 feet square, the walls and roofs of which are covered with boards. The soldiers have eaten up most of the horned cattle. hereabouts, but what few are left are very good eating. The houses are miserable. The inhabitants are mostly descendants of Hollanders, and for this reason the German language is pretty well known here. The house of Colonel von Donop belongs to a person named Koch from Hanau. I have seen quite a number of blacks, who are just as free as the whites. On the whole, nearly everything here is the same as with us at home—the same kinds of bushes and trees ; but as the soil is richer here, the leaves grow larger and the wood thicker. Staten-Island was during two months the only land in all North America which England held possession of ; that is, if I except Canada and New Scotland, her conquests during the last war.

Long-Island is a beautiful island. It has a great number of meadows, orchards, fruit-trees of all descriptions, and fine houses ; while cattle are still to be found in large numbers, notwithstanding the immense droves which the rebels carried off with them on their retreat. The inhabitants, with few exceptions, have deserted their residences. When we landed on the 22d of August we marched through Gravesend and New Utrecht, and the same evening we entered Flatbush. I made a sketch of Flatbush, as we were here five days, and during our stay we had several encounters with the rebels. It was a beautiful village before these cut-throats burned down the greater part of it. There are still standing, however, several country residences.

Newtown has several streets, Brookleein Kirk, etc., is a continuous, long street lined with trees and houses in close proximity to each other. Here are to be seen neat little houses surrounded by gardens, meadows, and fruit-trees of every variety. In Newtown are one Dutch Reformed and two English churches. Newtown includes Freshbone and Little Battein, both containing a few houses. Nearly all of the inhabitants of Freshbone are Quakers, who have a meeting-house. The Quakers are not rebels : on the contrary, they have publicly proclaimed in all of their gatherings and churches that whosoever went armed would lose their membership. In Jamaica-town there are three churches, viz., an English, a Presbyterian, and a Dutch Reformed. Quakers are not to be met with in this place. The market-town, " New-York ferry," is made up of a number of houses in a row, and mechanics and artisans are already beginning to thrive. I have made a sketch of it, because it is so nicely situated. The country around Jamaica is generally level and pleasant to the eye. From here a road leads to Hemstead, where lovely plains and patches of forest bordered by hillocks are to be seen. In fact, standing upon an elevation in the midst of the large and small Hemstead Plains, looking seaward towards the beach, the eye takes in one of the most charming landscapes imaginable. Hemstead is a "church village," having an English [i.e. Episcopal] and a Presbyterian church. It consists of a large extent of ground, although in Hemstead itself there are but few houses. The inhabitants are a rich and well-to-do people, as, indeed, are all the residents of Long-Island, for they possess a country's true wealth, viz., land. In fact, they are rich landed proprietors. A great many Quakers live here. Between Bush* and Newtown there are many houses, and also the village kirk,† which belongs to Newtown.

The boundaries between King's and Queen's counties have been incorrectly given upon all the charts, even on the one belonging to Holland. The northern boundary-lines begin at the ocean,‡ in the vicinity of

---

* Flatbush probably, though it might have been Bushwyck.

† Or "Krick." On account of the ink being very pale, it is difficult for me to make out all the proper names.—*Note by Schlözer. Kirk*, of course, is correct, and refers to the old Dutch church belonging to Newtown, and built about 1665. The first church built in N. Y. City was called "Gercformeede Kerch," and Governor Kief and three citizens were the first "kerk meesters." What a little bothered Schlözer, I suppose, was the fact that the word *Krick* (Newtown Creek) is met with a little further on.

‡ The writer wrote "ocean" purposely and not, as it might at first be inferred, through ignorance. In the journal of a Labadist (published in my "History of New York City"), who wrote intelligently of his visit to New York in 1679, occurs this minute: "The water by which it [Long Island] is separated from the Mahatans is improperly called the East River; for it is nothing else than an arm of the sea, beginning

Blackwell's Island ;* run through Krick,† with Newtown, Freshbone, Little Battein ‡ and Flushing on
the left; intersect the highway leading to Jamaica,
and end in an inlet on Jamaica Bay. I have cor-
rected these errors and the location of New Utrecht
upon my chart, and have made a new map of the
western part of Long-Island, comprising the counties
of Kings' and Queens'. The whole island forms an
exquisite picture. You can ride nearly an English
mile in these two counties without seeing a house.
The inhabitants are generally sprightly, and roguishly
inclined. The air here in September is most agreeable. Winter begins in December and ends with the
first or last of March. We often have heavy falls of

---

in the bay on the west and ending in the sea on the east.
After forming in this passage several islands, this water is as
broad before the city as the Y before Amsterdam, but the
ebb and flood tides are stronger."

  * It is really one mile south of that island.

  † This, of course, is Newtown Creek, or, as it was then
called, "Maspeth Creek." From the head of Maspeth Creek
the boundary ran "due south to certain marked trees on the
south side of the Hills;" then from "Newtown bounds at the
s.w. edge of the Hills ; the n.w. corner [of Jamaica] beginning at certain mark't trees at ye edge of ye said Hills, from
whence to run in a south line to a certain river, that is to the
east of Plunder's Neck, and bounded south by ye sea."

  ‡ Freshbone and Little Battein were small hamlets of
perhaps half a dozen houses, on the left bank of Maspeth or
Newtown Creek *going up*. They are now both within the
bounds of Long Island City.

snow, which furnishes good sleighing every year. Sometimes the winters are wet; but the summers are generally dry, except in the month of August, when thunder-storms are frequent. Tobacco is not cultivated in Kings' County, although it is in Jamaica. Every one living here enjoys in time of peace an agreeable, uniform, and healthy life. The horned cattle are strong and plentiful. The products of the garden are the same as with us at home. The ladies on this island are not ugly, and upon the mainland are even said to be pretty. The easy—in fact, I might say, the too easy—life these people led caused them to become overbearing; nevertheless, had it not been for the cabals in England, and especially in London, matters would not have been so bad as they are now. The more I look upon this country, with its lovely meadows, its bountiful crops of corn and hemp, and its beautiful fruit-gardens, the more I envy the former happy inhabitants of this excellent land, and the more I pity those unhappy ones who are now suffering from the intrigues and secret envy of their fellow-citizens. I saw barns filled with the treasure of the husbandman, but nowhere—or at least but seldom—did I meet with an inhabited house; for nearly all had been entirely destroyed by the war and the English. Peach and pear trees were more generally seen growing in the streets; but pear-trees were not so plentiful.

Blackwell's Island belongs to the island of New-York. It is a dull, barren piece of land, and is two English miles in length, by, in its widest part, a quarter of a mile broad. Free blacks live here, but there are in all only three houses. There are many blacks on New-York Island, but few of them are free.

On the north lies Bahama,* or Passon's Island, beautifully situated. It has meadows and fruit land, and some woods on the southwest side.

Still further north lies Belle † Island, also a lovely spot. It had only one house, and even this has been destroyed by the rebels. It lies just beyond Harlem, with Westchester on the other side. It belongs to a Captain Montrésor, of the English *corps du génie*, who remained with the army, and is therefore often called Montrésor's Island.‡

---

* Probably a misprint for *Buchanan's* Island, as it was called at that day. Schlözer—see note *ante*—says he was unable sometimes to make out the proper names in these letters.

† The " Bahama" and " Belle" Islands are now known as Ward's and Randall's Islands.

‡ "Captain John Montrésor [afterwards Colonel] purchased in 1772 an island near Harlem called Belle Isle. Since its purchase it has been known as Montrésor's and as Randall's Island. He and his family lived on it during the British ascendancy in New York, until all the buildings and outhouses were burnt."—*Introduction to the Journal of Captain John Montrésor.* The following is an entry in the above *Journal :* " 13th Jan. 1777 : This night (Monday) my House and out· houses, Barns and outhouses, on Montrésor's Island, formerly called Belle-Isle, and afterwards Talbot's Island, near Haerlem, and 8 miles from New York, was [*sic*] burnt by the Rebels." " Nov. 7th, 1772, is the date of the Deeds for Belle

The island of New York is the most beautiful island I have ever seen. No superfluous trunk, no useless twig, no unnecessary stalk, can here be found. Projecting fruitful hillocks, surrounded by orchards, meadows, and gardens full of fruit-trees, and single ones scattered over the hills, with houses attached, line both sides of the river, and present to the eye a beautiful scene. The houses, which are two stories high and painted white, are encircled by a piazza, and have

Isle, formerly Little Barn Island, and afterward Talbot's Island, and now purchased by me, John Montrésor, on the above day and year. The first grant of this Island, commonly known by the name of Little Barn Island, was by Richard Nicolls, Esqr., first Governor of New York, onto Thomas Delavall, Esqr., Collector and Receiver General of the Customs in these parts Feb. the 3d, 1667, in the 20th year of his Majesty's reign."

Captain John Montrésor was the eldest son of Colonel James Montrésor, who was Director-General of Engineers and lieutenant-colonel of the British army. Served under Abercrombie against Ticonderoga, and drew the plan of Fort Stanwix during the same summer—in 1759. In December, 1775, he (Captain John) was made by George III. "Chief Engineer of America." He was present in May, 1776, at, and acted as one of the managers of the celebrated ball called the " Mischianza" (gotten up by Major André), which was given by the British officers to Sir William Howe in Philadelphia, on the eve of his departure for England. " He had charge of the fireworks and ball-room decorations, and was accompanied on that occasion by Miss Auchmuty, one of the half-sisters of Mrs. Montrésor, whose mother had remarried the Rev. Samuel Auchmuty, D.D., of New York. He a weather-vane on top. They are also surrounded by beautiful walks, and are built and furnished in the best of taste. The Hudson has a strong current, and is salty fifteen miles inland.

So much for this time from one who is always on guard, watching, investigating, and writing at spare moments. One word more. You have heard of the Huguenot war in France? Well, what *there* was Religion, is *here* Liberty—fanaticism both!

---

was born April 6, 1736, at Gibraltar, and died at Portland Place, London, June 26, 1799. The name of Capt. Montresor, also, is associated, through Mrs. Rowson's book, with the ill-fated Charlotte Temple (Stanley), whom rumor assigned as his mistress. It is probable, however, that the story never had more foundation than that given it by the gossipy articles in the partisan newspapers of the day. Capt. Montrésor married at New York, March 1, 1764, Frances Tucker,—only daughter of Lieutenant Thos. Tucker of Bermuda, and a relative of Dr. Auchmuty, the rector, at that time, of Trinity Church,—by whom he had ten children.

LETTER FROM RHODE ISLAND.

[FROM A HESSIAN OFFICER TO HIS BROTHER.]

RHODE-ISLAND, June 24, 1777.

My last letter of April 5th from Portsmouth I hope you have received. I then informed you that Ensign —— and myself were together on the transport *Providence*, and that we would remain on that vessel until we reached America. In consequence, however, of Lieutenant —— being on board, who by his astounding bragging is the most unbearable man in the world, it was impossible for us to get along. We therefore changed our minds the day before our departure on the 5th of April, and went with our officers on board the transport *Lively*, where we found Ensigns —— and ——. On this vessel, besides having congenial companions, we had much more beautiful and commodious staterooms; and although the commander of the entire fleet had his separate sleeping-apartment, which took up much space, yet each of us also had his own sleeping-room, which could be locked; whereas on board the *Providence* there was but one room for our whole party.

On the 7th of April, after waiting in vain for our chasseurs, we weighed anchor at four o'clock in the morning and set sail ; our convoy being accompanied by the man-of-war *Somerset,* of 74 guns, on which was the English General ——* [Howe], who, it was

---

* General Howe. In this connection it is interesting—in these days of vandalism—to learn that the Billopp Manor-house on Staten Island, opposite Perth Amboy, is still (1891) standing. The residence is near Tottenville, and was erected by Colonel Billopp upon land granted to him by Queen Anne. During the Revolution Lord Howe used it for his headquarters at one time. The history connected with the place is curious. Lord Howe, as mentioned in the text, wished to confer with the " rebels," and to arrange a settlement of difficulties. Benjamin Franklin, John Adams, and Edward Rutledge were the committee chosen. Several letters were exchanged between Howe and Franklin in relation to a place of meeting, which was fixed finally at the " old Billopp house." It was then a two-days' journey from Philadelphia to Perth Amboy. The committee started, John Adams on horseback and Dr. Franklin and Mr. Rutledge in old-fashioned chairs. When they reached Perth Amboy Lord Howe's barge was there to ferry them across. He shook hands warmly with Franklin when he landed at Staten Island, and greeted the others cordially when Franklin introduced them. They all moved towards the house between lines of soldiery. One of the largest rooms of the Billopp mansion had been converted, with moss, vines, and branches, into a delightful bower, and there a collation of " good claret, good bread, cold ham, tongues, and mutton " was immediately served. After this Lord Howe opened the conference. He expressed his attach-

rumored, was empowered to make overtures of peace. There were, besides, ten transports with the 1260 Anspach troops on board.

On the 13th, a servant of an Anspach officer, having stolen a shirt from his master, and being afraid of punishment, jumped overboard. He was pulled out of the water dead.

On the 26th one of the wives of our chasseurs was confined.*

On the 2d of June we came in sight of land, a circumstance that caused a universal shout of joy.

On the 3d, at four o'clock in the afternoon, we entered the harbor of New York, and cast anchor near the city. I am forced to admit, judging by its exterior appearance, that I have never seen such a beautiful country as that which greeted our eyes on entering

---

ment to America and his gratitude for the honors bestowed upon his elder brother, who was killed at Lake George in the expedition against the French, eighteen years before, declaring that should America fall he should feel and lament it like the loss of a brother. Franklin bowed, and, smiling blandly, replied, " My lord, we will use our utmost endeavors to spare you that mortification." The conversation was conducted as among friends for four hours, but it amounted to nothing, except so far as it strengthened the patriots. The party separated with great show of courtesy, Howe saying, " I am sorry, gentlemen, that you have had the trouble of coming so far to so little purpose."

* The news that married couples were among the German troops in America is always useful [i.e., as a matter for future reference].—*Note by Schlözer.*

this harbor, where on the left was New Jersey and on the right New York Island.

On the 4th Ensign —— and I went into the city, and reported ourselves to General Heister. Now, to our great gratification, we, for the first time in many weeks, encamped on land, and with Auditor ——.

On the 5th all our baggage was brought from the vessels, and the regiments were quartered in an old church.* We also were obliged to spend a night in it, or rather among the tombstones, as we were unable to find another place for our equipage or any other shelter for ourselves—if a night in a graveyard could be called by that term. This experience gave us our first conception of what is meant by war in America!

On the 6th our recruits were drafted into the different regiments ; and we finally took up our quarters in the house of a rebel, that had been deserted by its owner.

By these details, my dear brother, you may in a faint degree judge of our present situation ; and that it is not now as it was in the last war, when the motto was, " Farmer, work, or thou wilt receive blows." In fact, let me tell you it is hard to live here. One is never sure of finding what he needs, and even should he be so fortunate as to stumble across it, it is terribly dear. In all my life I never heard of such high

---

* The old Dutch church corner of Nassau and Cedar Streets —afterward used as the Post-Office, and the site of which is now (1891) occupied by the Mutual Life Insurance Company.

prices. For instance, a loaf of bread (made of wheat, for corn is rarely raised here) and which at home costs one *albus*,* costs here 5 ; one pound of butter, 18 ; one pound of meat (mutton or beef), 10 ; a bottle of poor wine, 1 reichs-thaler ; one pound of snuff, 2 reichs-thaler and 8 silber-groschen ; a pair of boots, 20 gulden ; a yard of indifferent linen, 16 *albus;* a yard of the poorest woollen stuff, 1 reichs-thaler and 16 *albus*, etc., etc.

Now, in order to give you an idea of America, or, rather, that small portion which we still hold, I may not omit to say that it is really a beautiful, lovely land, and quite level. New York, especially, is one of the handsomest and pleasantest seaports I have ever seen ; although that part of the city which lies nearest the sea has been recently burned. The houses, which are in the English style, regular and well built, are not only of a palatial character, but are most elegantly furnished and papered inside. It is therefore a pity that this country, which, by the way, is exceedingly fertile, should be inhabited by such brutish people—people who have been brought into their present position by sheer luxury and extravagance, and who owe their downfall solely to their own haughtiness. Any one who is disposed to take their part, and to believe that they have sufficient cause to rebel, should for a time as a punishment live among them and become acquainted with their condition.

---

* An *albus* is a little less than a groschen.

Here a man, even of the meanest station, provided he will only do something, can live as well as the richest. Such a visitor would soon talk in a differ-ent strain, and would see, as I do, that it is not want, but frivolity and extravagance, that is the cause of this rebellion. Although the greater portion of the people are descended from wandering ragamuffins ousted from other places, yet they are so haughty here, and put on such airs, especially in New York, that their like cannot be found in the entire world. For example, the women—who, by the way, are nearly all good-looking, no matter whether they are the wives of shoemakers, tailors, day-laborers (of these there are very few, since nearly every one has a few negro slaves in his service)—are dressed in calico, muslin, and silk robes. This extravagance in dress, which daily increases, is caused by the inhabitants constantly taking in such large amounts of money from the troops; for no one would dream of taking a single grain of salt from them unless they paid them for it.

There is likewise nothing more vexatious than the fact that by an express order of the king the soldiers are obliged to treat this people, who are in reality all rebels, with the greatest courtesy—so much so, that not a grain of salt may be taken from them without compensation. The poor soldiers, accordingly, would die of starvation if the ship provisions were not furnished to them for 3 pence per *diem* (28 kellers), viz., one pound of zwieback [toasted bread or biscuit], salted but almost uneatable pork, a few musty peas, some oatmeal, and a little rum. With this diet they are forced to support life, although a good many are made sick by it.

On the 14th June, we (the recruits) embarked on a vessel bound for Rhode-Island, where one English and four German regiments are at present stationed.

On the afternoon of the 15th, we set sail, and passed on that day a place called Hell-gate—a spot fraught with the utmost danger to life and navigation.

On the 18th, we anchored off Newport-Island; on the 19th, I went to the town of Newport, the capital of Rhode-Island, and in great haste visited my sick brother; and on the 21st, we went into camp, which is four hours* distant from the city, at the end of the island, and directly opposite the rebels. This island is only four hours long by two broad, and is surrounded on all sides by the rebels, from whom it is only separated by a river three times as wide as the Werra. On this account, and also because they can fire shot almost into our camp, we are kept in a continual state of alarm. Again, as little or nothing is raised on the island in the way of vegetables—the inhabitants living chiefly on cattle—the outlook for us in the way of fresh provisions is very poor, especially as the rebels have taken with them all their live-stock. Meat costs here 12 *albus* a pound, while for a small mess of green peas (which will barely satisfy one person) we pay 7 silver groschen.

* In German the word " hour " is often used as a measure of distance, and signifies one league, i.e., five miles.

On the 23d of June (for having no tent I could not stay in the camp) I took up my quarters in a farm-house a quarter of an hour distant from the camp and near the water, in full range of the enemy's guns. The owner of the farm-house allowed me to occupy it more from fear that it might otherwise be taken possession of by English officers than through any courtesy to me. The farmer's name is Thomas Volkner, and his religion is that of a Baptist—a sect which is so numerous hereabout that its members cannot be counted. This sect does not have its children baptized. The greater portion of the inhabitants who are still here, however, are Quakers, who have neither the rite of baptism nor a minister. They accordingly go into a church and there wait for the Holy-Spirit to come and tell them what they shall say. If the Holy-Spirit fails to move them, which, by the way, happens very often, they silently return home, for they never sing.

On the 24th of June, two English officers made their appearance and proposed to occupy my room. As I was the prior occupant, however, they were unable either by threats or persuasions to accomplish their object, especially as I showed them the door with my drawn sword.

As regards the domestic products, they are the same as with us, the climate being similar except that it is much warmer. The garden vegetables are also exactly like ours, only the species are fewer in number. The trees, however, are somewhat different,—sassafras, cracknut, etc., which I have never before seen, being quite abundant.

As to animals, especially domestic ones, which I have more particularly observed, I find no difference, except that the horses are smaller and lighter, and are therefore fleeter and quicker in their movements. On the contrary, oxen and cows are nearly twice as heavy, and proportionately larger. Birds, excepting swallows, are different from ours, and twice as beautiful. There are neither sparrows nor moles in this place. With this I bring my letter to a close.

P. S.—In case any one should ask the reason why I have said nothing regarding the progress of the war, you can answer him that it is because I know no more about it now than I did when I left Germany, except those small skirmishes which signify little. So far as we know, nothing of consequence has taken place, except that the frigate *Unicorn* to-day brought in two rebel ships.

LETTER FROM A FIELD-CHAPLAIN.

NEW YORK ISLAND, Dec. 7, 1777.

The news of the capture of the two forts on Mud and Red-Bank in Delaware is no doubt known to you by this time, also the friendly reception of Burgoyne's army. Howe's and Washington's armies are stationed opposite each other at Philadelphia, the army of the latter having received considerable reinforcements.

It was here (New York) that several hundred people recently took an oath to fire the city and roast us, bag and baggage. Quite a large body of rebels were invited to cross the North River and look at the fun and see the roasting ! The kind Being who watches over the German and English armies, however, ordained it otherwise. He caused the secret plan to be unmasked, and without doubt the governor or his representative will be hung.

If the rebels keep their word, we may expect more visits from them, either here or in the vicinity. The two Anspach regiments are now in Philadelphia. They were, as I surmise from reading yesterday's paper, upon a cattle-hunting expedition under the command of Lord Cornwallis. Four thousand men brought 800 head into Philadelphia. Without doubt our esteemed field-chaplain will also have his share of the sheep, and I am the same as in Europe, etc.

DESCRIPTION OF THE COUNTRY
AROUND PHILADELPHIA
IN 1778.

AT PHILADELPHIA ON THE NECK, Jan. 18, 1778.
Your dear letter of the 25th of May, addressed to
'Lieutenant H. in New York, or Captain H. in
Philadelphia," reached me on the 4th of November.

My present ideas of America have greatly changed
from those that I expressed in my last letters. At
the present time I can form no mental picture of an
earthly paradise without including in it the Jerseys
and Long Island: not so, however, with Pennsylvania.
If the Hon. Count Penn were to offer me the whole
county of Pennsylvania, with the condition that I
should live here the rest of my life, I hardly think I
should accept it. And this is the land of promise—the
land where milk and honey flows, and which so many
have praised to us! You are doubtless aware that as
each North American province has hitherto main-

tained a separate existence and been governed by laws
of its own, it must be judged separately. The packet-
boat will start to-morrow : so now for a few hasty descriptions of the country and its climate.

Among one hundred people, not only in Philadelphia but in the entire vicinity, you will not find one
with a healthy color. This is caused by the unwhole-
some air and the bad water. In one way this cannot
be ascribed to the zone in which it lies, for Pennsylvania is in one of the healthiest : rather is it to be
attributed to the forests, morasses, and mountains,
which partly prevent the atmosphere from expanding
and in a measure poison the air, thus producing an
unhealthy climate. Nothing is more common than to
have a fever once a year, eruptions like the itch, etc.
Nor have I met anywhere with more crazy people
than in this town. Only yesterday, while dining with
a gentleman, a third person came into the room and
whispered in my ear, "Take care : this gentleman is a
madman !" The truth is, however, that nearly all of the
people are quietly mad—a sort of mental aberration
caused by a compression rather than a heating of the
blood. Very often the people are cured. One of
the reasons for this extraordinary state of things is
that none of the necessaries of life possesses the same
nutritious properties as our own. The milk, for
example, is not half as rich, and the bread contains
but little nourishment. The difference between the
quality of the food brought from Jersey and that from

Pennsylvania to the market in Philadelphia is very noticeable.

The cold in winter and the heat in summer are quite moderate, but the thunder-storms in summer and the moist ill-smelling air in the spring and autumn are unbearable. Should a heavy mist arise on a summer's morning, saturating everything with moisture, you may be sure of having a thunder-storm in the afternoon. If on a winter's morning you find the trees covered with frost, it will rain in the afternoon. Such phenomena, which are of daily occurrence, are only to be met with in this country.

As it is with vegetables here, which attain only half their growth, so it is with animals,—rabbits, partridges, peacocks, etc., being but half-grown ; while the meat of wild-game tastes like the flesh of domestic fowls.

One of the few good results of the war is the extermination of the forests, by which the air has become purer. One man named Hamilton, a resident of this city, cut down the trees on 1500 acres of land for the use of the hospital, and he had the patriotism not long since to make the remark in company, that "it was a very good thing for the land !" The fertility of the soil is such that two crops can be sowed and harvested yearly, but the fruit is not as good as with us. The greater part of America is rich in minerals, especially the strip in which we manœuvred last summer, viz., on the Elk River, Brandywine Cuik [Creek], Valley Hills, and the Schuylkill. There are plenty of trees. For instance, there are seven varieties of pine, without counting those belonging to the same species, viz., sassafras, cedars, and nut-trees, which, by the way, are what we generally burn on our hearths and camp-fires. The land, moreover, produces corn, wheat, oats, flax, hemp, Indian-corn, and potatoes— which, however, are not as good as those grown in Holland, although this is their mother-country. They also raise beets and garden vegetables of all kinds, but these do not attain the same size as ours. The fruits likewise are different. The grape cannot become thoroughly ripe on account of the mist I have before mentioned. Pears are scarce, and the apples lack flavor.

You have doubtless read in the newspapers about the stockades which cut up the land into so many sections that it is simply impossible for cavalry to manoeuvre on the plains. These defences, which are wooden palisades encircling acres of land, are put up as a protection against the cattle ; for every one turns his cattle (horses, sheep, cows, etc.) loose, without herders. After an acre has yielded its crops the farmer drives his cattle upon it,—alternating from one acre to another,—and hence each acre has its own palisades. However, an old German farmer living two miles from Philadelphia assured me that the one and a half feet of ground that would be lost by digging trenches and planting hedges would cost him more. Another reason why hedges are not planted is that they will not grow. The thornbush cannot be raised on account of an insect the name of which I have forgotten ; while the willow will not flourish every-where. At Hollander's Cuik I saw a newly planted grove of that tree.

Pigs are as fine in these parts as the best Holsteins, for the woods contain the best of mast, upon which those animals feed the entire year. Guinea-hens are abundant, though not as numerous as in the Jerseys and Long-Island. The Welsh-hen is classified as a wild bird, and can be found in the woods in flocks, like partridges. Sheep are plenty ; but as the farmer drives them into the forest he ruins their wool. Notwith-standing this, however, he sells the skins for 18 shil-lings in York money. Ducks and geese are the same and as good as with us, but no better. You cannot imagine the immense swarms of flies that are to be met with in this part of the world. Rabbits, black grouse, and partridges are only half as large as at home ; while bears and wolves may still be met with in Tol-pahaky,* 36 miles from Philadelphia, to which city those animals are often brought. A joint of bear's meat is a great delicacy.

There are also plenty of snakes. The large black

---

* Mr. J. G. Rosengarten, Jr., Dr. Charles O. Abbott, and Professor O. Seidensticker, of Philadelphia, courteously in-form me that the writer evidently refers to *Tulpehocken*, in Berks County, Pa.,—a name signifying "the place of the turtle,"—although the distance is given incorrectly, as it is much further. Bears are even now found within 36 miles of Philadelphia, on the west, north, and east, and in Southern New Jersey, and fifty years ago they were plentiful.

snake is yet found along the Schuylkill, as well as near our quarters. Only recently a farmer while chopping wood was chased by one of them, but a neighbor killed it with a club. Nothing, however, can be more terrible than the rattlesnake. Its length is from 12 to 16 feet; and its glance, the people living here believe, is capable of killing a person. Several years ago a farmer living in my neighborhood lost a relative in this manner. He had been hunting, and seeing a bear standing motionless before him, he took aim and laid him low. But scarcely had he reached the bear when he himself seemed transfixed, and then fell over *dead*. All this was caused by a rattlesnake that lay coiled up in a high tree. None are to be found nearer Philadelphia than Tolpahaky; though between Elk-Ferry and the head of the Elk, where we were quartered for three days, there were some. So much about the country. In my next letter I will give you the characteristics of the people, their culture, etc.

That the domestic animals are not as good as with us at home, may be accounted for by the habit the people have here of allowing them to roam at large during the winter and summer.

Recently I wrote you that no white glass was manufactured in America. In Manheim (Pennsylvania), however, a factory was started two years before the war. This factory, in common with the porcelain factories, —in fact, all the arts and industries,—seem to be prostrated, and all on account of the high wages.

Do you wish to know where I am living? If so,

take a translation of "Barnaby's Travels,"* open it at page 90, and read: "from here the road leading to the city was lined with country-seats, pleasure-gardens, and orchards in full bloom." Among these "country-seats, pleasure-gardens, and orchards" the highly-praised rifle corps have their quarters; and here, upon the Schuylkill, midst the scenes that Barnaby describes, I intend to do picket duty to-morrow. It seems to me that this sketch is plainer than that drawn by many an engineer.

---

* Andrew Barnaby, an English divine, born 1732 at Ashfordby, Leicestershire; died March 9, 1812. He came to America soon after 1757, and, in 1776, published "Travels through the Middle Settlements of North America, in 1759–60." In 1786 he was preferred to the Archdeanery of Leicester. He also wrote a volume of sermons, and a "Journal of a Tour to Corsica in 1766."

LETTER FROM PHILADELPHIA.

PHILADELPHIA, May 7, 1778.

Excuse me for writing so briefly at this time. It is very warm to-day, and to-morrow our gracious friend sets sail.

You can, however, obtain further details of our present situation from the enclosed.* So far as can be seen, things are about in the same condition as when I last wrote. We are quietly sitting here and awaiting events.

Meanwhile, the lovely summer is approaching, which will have the effect, perhaps, of making it pretty hot for both armies. How you will be pleased with the exquisite German in the *State Courier!* Our loved mother-tongue is completely Anglicized in this colony, and will soon be transformed into what may be called "the Pennsylvania language," which will be unrecognizable by either Germans or English.

---

* This was a copy of a Philadelphia newspaper for Wednesday, the 6th May, 1778, called *The | Pennsylvania State Courier | of current | Weekly News. |* Published by Christopher Saur, Jr., and Peter Saur, in Second st., Philadelphia. It contains accounts of many atrocious incidents then happening, which are not here given, as the file can be referred to.

Up to the present time my experience here makes me well contented. My landlord is an arch rebel, an apothecary, and a native of Nuremburg. He swears that I will have to stay in Philadelphia, and demonstrates to a hair's-breadth that the king is a tyrant. The city is beautiful, the country agreeable, and the inhabitants are good fellows for your money.

We hear that Mr. [General] Putnam was lately tried before a court-martial and honorably acquitted of all charges brought against him. The principal one was leniency towards prisoners—a sentiment he seems to have imbibed years ago, when he had the honor to serve his Majesty for several years in the late [French and Indian] war.

From Chester we have received the following news, which it is believed is true. At the beginning of this week two men had caught a good mess of fish and were dividing them in a ware-house near the water front, when two horsemen rode up and inquired of a woman living near by what they were doing? While the woman was still talking with them, one of the men had put his share of the fish into a cart and was driving away, when one of these heroes rode up to him and asked where he was going with the fish? The answer was, " Home." Whereupon, the rider rode up to the man and without any hesitation shot him dead on the spot; and so close was he to the poor fellow, that the flash from the pan of his pistol set his coat on fire. Meanwhile his companion rode up to the ware-house where the other unfortunate fisherman had remained with his fishes, and cursing him for a Tory, shot him down also, although surrounded by a number of children.

We have also received verified news from Whitpaine Township, Philadelphia County, that a certain preacher of the Reformed Church, named Wickel, who had formerly held forth in Bohemian and Wenzen* churches, has recently given up preaching and turned street foot-pad. As a preacher he had been in the habit of wickedly reviling the king and his government, and had likewise exhorted his hearers to remain steadfast to the rebellion and to turn street robbers. (His recompense, no doubt, will be great.) Whether his congregation did not obey him in everything, whether he became jealous that others became rich by following his éxhortations while he remained poor, or whether he desired to learn and do both things himself, is not known. Let it suffice to say that this " buck" waylays people on the roads to and from the city, and relieves them of their valuables. Take care of yourself, and believe me, etc.

---

* The Wenzens, who are descendants from the Sclave tribe of Wendts, are a sect near Berlin, which for several hundred years have preserved their own peculiar forms of worship, customs, habits, costumes, etc., unchanged. They are Lutherans in religion. Their dress—especially that of the women—is exceedingly picturesque. It consists of short petticoats of various brilliant colors, and a white cap with large flaps standing out like wings on either side. They never marry out of their own sect.

DESCRIPTION OF PHILADELPHIA, ITS PEOPLE, ETC.

[FROM CAPTAIN H.]

ON THE NECK AT PHILADELPHIA, June 2, 1778.

Several weeks ago, the army being ordered to put on board the ships their unnecessary baggage, I sent, among other articles, all my books, journals, charts, sketches, and note-books. For this reason you will not in this letter receive anything from me in relation to my winter campaign.

Philadelphia is, in its way, a very pretty city. Ninety-four years ago not a house was to be seen, and now there are between twenty-five hundred to three thousand. Indeed the fire-insurance companies have policies on 1993. This will give you an idea of the growth of the place. The rectangular streets and the sameness of the houses—which, as a rule, are but two stories high, though a few are three stories—present a laughable appearance. After we had had possession of the city for four weeks, and when the vessels arrived from New York, everything put on such a bustling air, that, as the inhabitants said, one would not have known the city in time of peace. Two out of every three houses contain shops (not shops like those in Hamburg), but similar to those of G—sche. A broad stone placed at the side [front] of the houses makes walking very comfortable ; and I must acknowledge that the arrangement of the streets is better than in Göttingen, The gutters do not empty directly upon the stones; consequently, in rainy weather, when you need these stones the most, you are not compelled to leave the sidewalks and wade about in the middle of the street. In the summer almost every householder stretches a piece of canvas across two upright poles placed on the street, and thus you are enabled to walk in the shade.

The merchant, or rather the shopkeeper, whose trade formerly was confined within narrow limits, is a laughable creature. He can only be compared with the librarian of a circulating library. For instance, should certain wares be in fashion and have a great sale in England, he will push them in Philadelphia, although he may know nothing about them! Recently, while walking in Second Street, I ran across a tobacco-dealer who had painted on a swinging-sign a German and English inscription. The English one read as follows : " Tobacco sold here as good as the best imported ;" while the German one read: " Tobacco sold here as good as the best of English."

Mechanics and artisans are very scarce. The ablest mechanics are hatters, shoemakers, and tailors. Of artisans, the best, and I may say the only ones, are saddlers and goldsmiths. Workers in ivory, steel, iron, stucco-work, bone, embroidery, silk, gold and silver ware are entirely unknown. All of those articles are sent on here by the English ; and, in fact, whatever they choose to send is most welcome.

In connection with all of this I may mention the unbearable self-conceit of the Americans, and especially the Philadelphians, who imagine that no country is more beautiful, fortunate, rich, or prosperous than their own ; and this, too, although it is still in its infancy. The reason for this scarcity of mechanics and artisans is easily given. Wages are so high that goods cannot be sold at a price sufficiently remunerative to get back the outlay of money for work performed. A man, for instance, importing goods from England can therefore sell more cheaply than a merchant here manufacturing his own goods. Why workmen's wages are so high can also be explained. Journeymen are difficult to be obtained simply because they can make a more agreeable and easy living by following agriculture. If a man works three hours a day at the latter occupation, he has twenty-one hours remaining in which he can sleep, yawn, breakfast, promenade, gossip, etc. He cannot, however, lead this blissful life in the workshop.* You can therefore judge for yourself what

---

* Compare the above with *Genovesi Burgerl., Œknonomic*, p. 139, chapter 15. This explanation seems to make clear why among the ancient Hebrews, where agriculture was in a most flourishing state, the fine-arts did not seem to prosper. Every Pennsylvanian can easily become a farmer or a

the future of American culture will be. As long as there is enough land to be had the peasant will not become an artisan.*

---

landed proprietor ; and every Hebrew was obliged to be one according to the Mosaic laws.—*Note by Schlözer.*

* In this respect, times seem to be greatly changed. *Now* our farms are nearly deserted, and large portions of the land untilled, because farmers' sons rush to the cities for employment, no matter of what kind, so long as they can be residents of a *city*—seemingly the height of their ambition.

LETTER FROM RHODE ISLAND.

NEWPORT, RHODE ISLAND, Sept. 8, 1778.

We are now in an extremely deplorable, and, in fact, a very dubious situation; and at present our only pleasure consists in receiving news from home. Since the 29th of July, on which day the French fleet appeared off the harbor and landed 25,000 rebels on the island, we have been in a most desperate state of mind. We supposed as a matter of course that we should be taken prisoners; and although, thank God, we have been spared that misfortune, our prospects in regard to fresh vegetables and meat are very uncertain. We need not expect any fresh food whatever for at least fourteen days; and meanwhile we will have to exist on dried peas, rice, and salt provisions. We wish most heartily that we could leave this island and again see Germany. In the last engagement we lost in Hessians 105 men in killed, wounded, and prisoners.*

---

* The engagement here referred to was the action of Quaker and Turkey-Hill, which occurred on the 29th of August, 1778. An attempt by the British to gain the rear of the Americans and cut off their retreat brought on a general action, in which from twelve to fifteen hundred of the latter were engaged. The British line " was finally broken, after a severe engagement, in attempts to take the redoubt on the American right ; and they were driven back in great confusion to Turkey-Hill, leaving many of their dead and wounded on the field." The American loss was thirty killed and one hundred and thirty-two wounded, and forty-four missing. The British lost in killed and wounded two hundred and ten, with twelve missing. According to the above writer, therefore, exactly half of this loss was borne by the Hessians. " Lossing's Field-Book of the Revolution" contains an excellent picture of the scene of this engagement, from a print in the *Gentleman's Magazine.*

LETTER FROM SAVANNAH.

SAVANNAH IN GEORGIA, Jan. 16, 1779.

You have, I suppose, received my last letter from New York. In it I announced the fact that I had been ordered on board, together with those who had received their discharge from the regiments of Von Wöllwarth and Von Wissenbach. Now, however, I am prepared to give you a short description of this route of ours, or, rather, of my fourth sea-voyage.

Every one can understand that it is quite disagreeable to go promenading upon the ocean—especially at a time of year like the present. On the 6th of November we embarked ; and on the 8th, we sailed from New-York for Stäten-Island. Here had gathered the fleet, which consisted of between 46 to 50 vessels. Among them were a war-ship named " Phœnix," carrying 44 guns, and commanded by Commodore Hyde Parker, Jr.; the 24-gun frigate, " Fowey ;" the " Vigilant," having the same number of guns, but consisting of 18-'and 24-pounders ; a row-galley (*Ruder-Galere*), and other variously armed sloops. The troops were commanded by Lieutenant-Colonel Campbell of the 71st

Scottish Regiment ; and the entire corps consisted of about 3500 men, which make up the following regiments, viz., the above-mentioned 71st Regiment, of two battalions ; Wöllwarth and Wissenbach, of the two battalions of Langry ; the third battalion of Skinner; and the New York Volunteers. The last-mentioned is a corps only recently organized in America. Wöllwarth's regiment filled three vessels, viz., the "Alicia," on which were one major, three lieutenants, two ensigns, one regimental-quartermaster, and 200 men, and myself ; the "Union," and the "Venus." Wissenbach's filled the "Nancy," "Howtown," and the "Minerva."

On the 12th November, as soon as the necessary orders regarding the signals and the disembarking, etc., had been distributed, we weighed anchor, and about one o'clock in the afternoon got under way, wind and weather being good. About five o'clock in the afternoon we again cast anchor at Sandy Hook, near the light-house. While riding at anchor we encountered on the 13th, a strong wind, which so increased in violence on the 14th and 15th, and caused such havoc among the fleet, that the commander was obliged on the 16th, to sail back again to Staten-Island with the entire fleet. A number of vessels lost their anchors; two of them were driven out to sea; and one was dashed to pieces on the shore. The ship "Howtown" lost her bowsprit, through colliding with another vessel which had also lost her fastenings during the night, and both were only separated with much difficulty.

During all this trouble a number of Scots were drowned. The " Alicia" lost only her anchor. We now had to ride at anchor until everything had been put to rights. Wissenbach's men meanwhile were taken from the " Howtown," and put on board the ship " Friendship." The " Betsey," which had been driven ashore, was again got afloat ; but as she was damaged, another vessel took her place. During this interval Regimental Quartermaster K—— and myself started to spend several days in New York, astonishing our friends by our appearance, as they believed that by this time we were far out at sea.

On the 27th of November, everything had again been made "ship-shape ;" and on the same day the frigate " Roebuck" and a large East-Indiaman with four other ships joined us. On the " Roebuck " was Lord Carlisle, and on the Indiaman, William Eden, Esq., of whom, perhaps, you may have heard something in Göttingen. Both are royal commissioners, who have been sent over here to make overtures of peace. The rebels, however, will have nothing to do with them.

To-day, the 27th November, we left Sandy Hook, where we arrived last evening. Up to the 31st, we were so fortunate as to have a favorable wind, with only occasional rough weather. On the 1st of December we had beautiful and in fact extraordinarily warm weather. Towards evening a very fierce wind arose, since which time we have had such violent storms, that especially on the third day out, one could neither hear nor see anything occurring around us. It was indeed terrible. We could fasten nothing securely; trunks and portmanteaus were thrown about promiscuously; while each moment you were in danger of being thrown out of bed and dashed against the floor. For fourteen days we were unable to sleep, nor could we during that time either eat or drink anything in a decent manner. We also cut many comical figures, and presented, I doubt not, many ludicrous postures, before we were able to restore our equilibrium. It was indeed funny ! With one arm you held on to the bedstead, at the same time reeling around like a drunken man. Meanwhile, the rain continued incessantly; and, as we drew nearer the south, the weather became so unbearably warm that we were obliged to open all of our windows [port-holes] and strip ourselves to the skin. The sea appeared at one time all mountains and at another all valleys, the foam giving them the appearance of being constantly covered with a mantle of snow; while the waves seemed to fight among themselves as to which should be the first to dash against and overwhelm our ship. It was indeed most terrific—the sailors themselves saying that they, in all their experience, had never seen the like. With each succeeding storm some of the vessels disappeared from view, a circumstance that obliged us to lay-to for a day or two till they were again in sight; and in the midst of this dreadful gale one of the wanderers finally made her appearance. But, notwithstanding all this, most of us continued well and in good spirits; and, occasionally, we were favored with very laughable scenes as we saw the actions of the women and soldiers.

At last, on the 16th of December, the commodore signalled for a pilot. We found ourselves in forty fathoms of water, which already looked darker than sea-water. A violent wind again arose on the 17th, driving us and ten other ships (one of which had on board the agent of the fleet) away from the convoy, towards the land, which our sailors spied from the mast-head. It was the coast of Carolina, not far from Charlestown [Charleston]. The rebels also may have discerned our fleet; for hardly had we turned about to search for the missing vessels when thick columns of smoke shot up into the air at several places. These are their signals when they expect an enemy. In the evening we again came up with our convoy, which still consists of 38 ships.

Up to the 20th, the wind and weather were fair, though very warm. To-day we bought a pig from the captain of our ship for six guineas. It weighed 120 pounds. We at once made some very good Hessian sausages, and also regaled ourselves with pudding-broth.

The 21st, we again saw land, but still in the vicinity of Carolina. On the 23d we arrived in the neighborhood of Georgia, and at last, about five o'clock in the evening, cast anchor quite deeply into the sea, in eleven fathoms of water. On the 24th, we weighed anchor and sailed towards the Savannah River, which we at first took to be Port-Royal. Soon afterwards we saw the light-house, and about one o'clock in the afternoon we anchored, and were safe from all storms. The rebels, who were in possession of the city of Savannah, again made their usual signals. On the 26th, a number of vessels, which had been driven away from the fleet while at sea, arrived. We learned that a ship which had been driven from Sandy Hook to sea had entered the St. John's River in Florida, and had lost all her masts in a storm. Two ships having horses on board, and which had been driven away during the second storm, and that every one supposed to be lost or captured, are said to have arrived at St. Augustine.

On December 28th, orders were given to disembark. Accordingly, about twelve o'clock, we sailed up the Savannah River towards the city, but on account of the ebb-tide we anchored about 6 miles from Savannah. On the 29th, the troops were carried on flatboats towards the city, and landed not far from it. Meanwhile, the rebels had posted themselves upon elevations and in houses, and a Scottish captain was immediately killed. The enemy, which mustered not more than 800 men, were commanded by a general named Howe. They did not, however, make a long stand. Our loss was 20 killed and wounded, among whom were two of Wöllwarth's men. The rebel loss consisted of 80 killed and wounded, and 400 prisoners. Their leader, General Howe, with the survivors started up the Savannah River towards Ebenezer. Twelve cannon, a large number of magazines, and several ships (among them a French vessel carrying 22 guns) were captured. The regimental quartermaster and myself remained upon the ship.

On the 31st, we started for the city, and took possession of advocate Farley's house, in which we found a fine library.

Savannah, now forty years old, lies in latitude 32°, and has about 600 houses, for the most part lightly built. The chief commerce of the inhabitants—of whom, by the way, few could be seen—is rice, indigo, and sago. Most of the inhabitants had run away with the rebels, and had as a general thing either buried their valuables or taken them into the interior of the country. The finest furniture, counters of banking-houses, mahogany tables and chairs, were smashed into bits and lay scattered about the streets. Indeed, it was a most pitiful sight. Within gunshot of the city is a handsome barrack built by the rebels. In it the Hessian regiments are quartered. No stones can be seen here—nothing, in fact, but white sand. The latter is piled up so high that in going through it you experience the same feeling as if you went through fallen snow a foot deep. At the present time (January) it is so warm that no fire is needed; and in summer—as we are informed by the inhabitants, who are now coming in with their arms—it is so hot that they boil eggs in the sand, and sometimes can even roast meat in it. No mountains are to be seen, much less a plain—nothing, in fact, but dense woods. The trees yield turpentine and pitch. We are now eating early vegetables, such as beans, peas, lettuce, and white and yellow turnips. Wild ducks, geese, turkeys, pheasants, parrots, large and small game, as well as domestic fowls, are plentiful. Bears, wolves, tigers,* and similar wild beasts are also met with. Buffaloes, likewise are to be found in the forests further inland. Rattle-snakes and even more deadly animals abound, and are, as you may well imagine, most disagreeable. I will at some future time tell you all about them when we are together face to face. The variable cold, and then suddenly the excessive hot weather, together with the numerous morasses and stagnant water, are the cause of many diseases, especially fevers. Three and four years in succession, and in fact one may say every year up to the fortieth, the inhabitants (they seldom live longer) have fevers. Many Germans hereabout attain, however, a great age. I have indeed met with several who are 74 and 80 years old. This, you see, still gives one some consolation.

The English General Prevost† is daily expected with his garrison from St. Augustine. They are the 162d and 60th Regiments of Royal Americans, consisting of four battalions. Herr von Porbeck and many Germans are with them, and among others an old university friend of mine, the son of the G. R. H.,

---

* " Tiger " is the word in the original. The writer, however, probably had in his mind panthers or cougars.

† It may give one some idea of the way in which old times are linked with the present, to state that a nephew of this same general is still (1891) living, a clerk in the N. Y. Custom-house.

from Jena, as a lieutenant. He is married, and his wife arrived here yesterday. She is also from Jena, and in my time was still a young woman. The English regiments are stationed at Ebenezer, 25 miles from this city. The Salzburgers are also stationed at this place. We are in sight of Charlestown, though it is fully 120 miles distant from us here, and 190 miles from St. Augustine. It is thought that we will not reach the former city, although it was so given out on our departure from New York. May Heaven grant it!—much as I desire to see new places. The above-mentioned Madame H—— gives no good account of it; still, it is healthier than here, as it is more hilly, and situated nearer the sea.

N. S.—General Prevost has this moment arrived with 250 horsemen. They were farmers, who had banded together in this province and that of Carolina, having taken sides with the king, and for this reason had been pursued by the rebels and driven into the wildernesses. Finally, they retreated into a swamp (or, rather, an island surrounded by marshes), where the rebels were unable to reach them. Here they lived for six days on roots and herbs, until they were rescued by General Prevost. They all wore red bands upon their hats, which denote that they are friends of the king. They looked ragged, and wore shoes of untanned skins. Every one carried a musket before him upon his horse. They are fast being drilled into regular soldiers, and have received green riding-waistcoats with black collars and trimmings.   S. D. H——u, *Auditeur.*

MAJOR-GENERAL STEUBEN TO PRIVY-COUNSELLOR BARON DE FRANK IN HECHINGEN.*

In Camp at New Winsor, on the North River,
July 4, 1779.

This, my friend, is the fifth letter I have sent you from this part of the world. As I have as yet received no answer to any of them, I am apprehensive that my letters have failed to reach you. Two ships on which I forwarded letters to Europe I see have been seized by the English; and in regard to the fate of two other vessels, in which I sent letters to you and to another friend, I am uncertain. Your silence, my dearest friend, makes me feel that these have also been lost. As I am sending this present letter through the French Minister Plenipotentiary, M. Gerard, I am hoping—in fact, flattering myself—that it will come

---

* This letter purports to be given in the appendix to, Kapp's " Life of Steuben ;" but not only is it not rendered in full, but many delicate touches, revealing the personal traits and affectionate and kind-hearted disposition of the man, are entirely omitted. Besides, considerable of the letter which is given is a paraphrase, and not a translation.

239

to hand. I will again repeat as far as possible what I have already substantially stated in a former letter.

My first letter to you, my dearest friend, was written from Boston about five weeks after my arrival in this part of the world. You will find a better description of a storm in "Robinson Crusoe" or other tales of strange adventure than I am able to give you. I will only say this much—that I have gone through two storms, each of which were of the very roughest description. The first storm we met with was in the Mediterranean Sea, near the coast of Africa; and the other one was near the coast of New Scotland [Nova Scotia]. Each lasted three days, and in both of them, but especially the first one, my frigate was damaged to such an extent that even our sea-officers gave up all hope. If you will add to these small inconveniences, the fact that the forepart of the ship took fire three times, and that we had 1700 cwt. of powder on board; and, furthermore, that a mutiny among the sailors placed us in the dilemma of having to enter into an engagement with 14 men against 84 in order to overpower the ringleaders; and that it took us sixty days to make the voyage, in the most dangerous time of the year— you will then see that this passage was one of the most dangerous and dreadful that could be imagined!

But disagreeable as my voyage had been, so was my landing in America most flattering. We anchored off Portsmouth, the chief town and capital of New Hampshire, on the 1st December, 1777. Before entering the harbor I sent my secretary in a sloop to the

commandant to announce my arrival. General Ladom* himself, who was in command, came on board
the ship, and took my officers and myself away in his
barge. Upon my arrival in the harbor the guns of
the fort and all of the ships lying at anchor were discharged in my honor ; and some thousand of the inhabitants upon my landing welcomed me in the most
friendly manner. M. Ladom conducted me to his
house, where we dined ; and meantime all the people
came running up to gaze on me, as if I were a rhinoc-
eros ! †

Greatly as I had been weakened by my painful
voyage, I yet devoted the next day to an inspection
of the fortifications. The third day I reviewed the
troops of the garrison, and on the 4th of December I
continued my journey to Boston by land. ‡

---

* John Langdon, a true patriot and soldier, who was at
Bennington, Saratoga, and Rhode Island. He was a delegate
to Congress, and also to the convention that formed the
Federal Constitution. In 1788 he was chosen governor of
New Hampshire; and from 1789 to 1791 served as U. S.
Senator. In 1812 a majority in Congress selected him for
Vice-President of the United States, an honor which he
declined. He was born at Portsmouth, N. H., 1739, and
died Sept. 18, 1819.

† An American of the present day would have written,
"all the people came running up 'to see the elephant.' "

‡ An amusing anecdote of General Steuben is minutely related in Kapp's "Life of Steuben," which occurred on this
journey to Boston. A Tory landlord of a tavern in Worcester County, Mass., having declared that he had neither beds

My reception in Boston was as flattering as that in Portsmouth. Here I met the celebrated Mr. Hancock, the former President of Congress. He showed me an order, just received from Congress, to the effect that all the requisite conveniences for the journey of myself and suite to Yorktown—where Congress at that time was assembled—should be arranged to my satisfaction. Mr. Hancock himself undertook the management ; and, as a consequence, wagons, sleighs, and led and off horses were furnished me. Five Moors [negroes] were given me as grooms and wagon-servants, and also a commissary to look after quarters and forage while upon the journey. Moreover, as I had brought along only one *valet de chambre* and one cook from Paris, I engaged two Englishmen in Boston as servants, and likewise formed a field equipage for myself and officers. From here (Boston) I wrote my first letter to you, in which I enclosed one for his Highness the Prince,* and a packet to Captain von H——; and as far as I can now remember, there was also a letter to Fr——.

The preparation of my equipage [outfit] detained me over five weeks in Boston ; but finally, on the 10th January, 1778, I continued my journey to Yorktown. At this place Congress received me with every imag-

---

nor provisions for the party, Steuben levelled his pistol at the man's head, and demanded both. They were quickly furnished, and in the morning the Baron liberally rewarded his host in Continental money.

* The Prince of Hohenzollern-Hechingen.

inable distinction.   A house had already been prepared for me, and two sentries were placed before the
door of my dwelling.   The day after my arrival Congress sent a committee of three of its members to
wait on me, to learn under what conditions I would
enter the service of this country.   My answer was,
that I was unwilling at present to make any terms
with Congress; that I desired first to go through the
approaching campaign as a volunteer; that I only
asked for commissions for those officers who composed
my suite; and that I did not wish to take either rank
or pay.   This was acceded to by Congress, as I had an-
ticipated would be the case.   I received also a letter of
acknowledgment couched in the most complimentary
terms, and stating among other things that I should
be deferred to in every particular.*   My officers received their brevets, and even my secretary was given
the rank and pay of a captain.

At this stage I must mention that no higher rank
than that of a major-general is designated in our military rank here.   General Washington is the oldest

---

* In Kapp's translation this sentence is not only para-
phrased but incorrectly rendered.   Kapp makes Steuben say
that Congress sent him a " Resolution of Thanks," whereas
the Baron says they sent him a "letter of acknowledgment"
—a very different idea.   Perhaps this is not of much consequence; only, if the letter is worth giving at all, it should
be translated accurately.   As a matter of fact, Congress did
pass a resolution of thanks; only Steuben does not here
say so.

major-general, and as general-in-chief all the prerogatives of a general field-marshal in other armies are accorded him. His authority is as undisputed as that of the Stadtholder of Holland was in the zenith of his power. The other major-generals, whose numbers at the present time do not exceed nine, command corps, armies, wings and divisions. Major-General Gates commands the Army of the North, General Lincoln that of the South, and General Sullivan the forces against the Indians. All are subject to the orders of the general-in-chief. The second rank is that of brigadier-general. These command brigades, the same as major-generals in European armies.

Upon my arrival at the army I was again received with more marks of distinction than I had expected. General Washington came some miles to meet me and accompanied me to my quarters, where I found an officer and 25 men on guard. On my remonstrating against this on the ground that I was simply to be regarded as a volunteer, he replied in the most courteous manner that the entire army took pleasure in protecting such volunteers. He presented Major-General Lord Stirling and several other generals to me, and also Lieutenant-Colonel Fernans * and Major Walker,† whom Congress had designated as my ad-

---

* Ferrand, Marie Louis, Baron and Count de, Governor of Santo Domingo, born in Besançon, France, 12th October, 1753; died in Palo Hincado, Santo Domingo, November 7, 1808.

† Walker, Benjamin, a favorite aide of Baron Steuben, born

jutant-generals. On the same day my name was given to the army as the password, and on the following day the army turned out, General Washington accompanying me to review it. In a word, if Prince Ferdinand of Brunswick or the first field-marshal of Europe had arrived in my place he could not have been received with more marks of distinction than I was.

My services as a volunteer lasted no longer than five weeks, during which I drilled the army and made various dispositions in it which met with such approbation that I received my commission as a major-general on the 26th of April. This was also accompanied at the same time with another commission of inspector-general of all the armies of the United States. My salary was now fixed at 16,400 French

---

in England in 1753; died in Utica, N. Y., 13th January, 1818. As stated in the text, he was at this time aide-de-camp to Baron Steuben, and in 1781-2 to General Washington. He was Naval Officer of New York under Washington's Administration, and Representative in Congress from New York in 1801-3. In 1797 he was agent of the vast estates of the Earl of Bute in Central New York, and was identified with the progress and growth of Utica.

The late Mrs. Almy W. Rogers, the mother-in-law of Mr. Wm. S. Mersereau and of Mr. Charles W. Miller of New York City, was a ward of Col. Benjamin Walker. The tea-cup used by that General as part of his breakfast equipage is now in the possession of her daughter, Mrs. Miller, by whom it is cherished as a most precious relic. In these iconoclastic days it is pleasant to put on record a fact of this kind.

livres ;* while, in addition, my table and all of my official staff † were maintained free of cost by a commissary of our own, and furnished with everything needful. Moreover, 22 horses for myself and equipage, 1 captain of horse, 2 lieutenants, and 40 dragoons to act as a body-guard were assigned to me by Congress. Furthermore, my adjutants and officers received the requisite number of horses and servants commensurate with their rank. I have 2 adjutant-generals, 2 inspection-adjutants, and 2 secretaries whose salaries are paid by Congress. Moreover, I have as adjutants Major des Epiniers, a nephew of the celebrated Beaumarchais, and the Marquis de Brittine, a major in the service.

Flattering as these decided marks of distinction have been, it only, my friend, makes me the more desirous to merit them. As far as my mental faculties and bodily vigor will allow, I shall unremittingly devote them to fulfilling the demands of a nation which has honored me with such great confidence. No difficulties, no troubles, no danger, shall, nor can they,

---

* About $3300.

† Steuben in one of his letters gives the number of his staff as twenty-one. They were Majors De Romanai, De L'Enfant, and Des Epiniers ; Captains Duponceau (who was also his first secretary) and De Pontière ; Colonels Walker and Fleury ; Lieutenant-Colonel Ternant ; Captains Duval and Fairlie ; Major North ; Colonel Wm. S. Smith ; Lieutenant-Colonel N. Fish ; Colonel Meade ; Messrs. Peyton, Randolph, and Moore ; Majors Galvan, Villefranche, Barber, and Popham ; and lastly, Lieutenant-Colonel de la Lanyanté.

prevent my success. My department is extensive, and one eighth of the world seem to think that my talents may be of service to them. Thank God that up to the present they have been; and cheerfully will I die for a nation that has so highly honored me with its confidence. Up to the present time all of my undertakings have progressed successfully, and I can say that the trust reposed in me by the army increases daily. I commanded the left wing in the first engagement of the battle of Monmouth last year, and was so fortunate as to turn the day in our favor ; and in all the smaller engagements, both of the last and present campaigns, I have been lucky enough to have all the soldiers anxious to be under my command.*

---

* At the battle of Monmouth Steuben rallied the retreating and demoralized troops of General Lee. He commanded in this battle, as he says, the left wing; and Alexander Hamilton, who witnessed the veteran-like action of the troops under Steuben, said he " had never known till that day the value of discipline." " Baron Steuben," also writes General Scammell, in a letter dated at Valley Forge, April 8, 1778, to General Sullivan, " sets us a truly noble example. He has undertaken the discipline of the army, and shows himself to be a perfect master of it, not only in the grand manœuvres but in the most minute details. To see a gentleman dignified with a lieutenant-general's commission from the great Prussian monarch condescended [sic] with a grace peculiar to himself, to take under his direction a squad of ten or twelve men in the capacity of drill-sergeant, commands the admiration of both officers and men, and causes them to improve exceedingly fast under his instructions."

Last winter I completed the " Infantry and Cavalry Tactics," which were at once printed and promulgated.

Congress testified its thanks to me, both by a letter of acknowledgment, which was published in all the newspapers, and by a present of two saddle-horses and 4000 thalers (a thaler is 5 livre and 10 sous) ; and not only my adjutants, but even my secretaries, received gratuities.

The winter I passed in Philadelphia. On the 4th of January, I was appointed a member of the Directory of War [War Department] ; and on the 26th of March I set out to join the army. During my stay in Philadelphia I formed an intimate acquaintance with the French Minister, M. Gerard, whose departure I deeply regret. He honored me by coming in person to the camp to visit me ; and I need not say that he was received by the army with all the honors due an ambassador. The day following his arrival I ordered a manœuvre to be executed by eight regiments of infantry and 16 cannon ; and at the close M. Gerard, the general-in-chief, and all the generals and colonels of the army dined with me at a table consisting of sixty covers.

I am at present on a tour of inspection for the purpose not only of reviewing all the regiments, but of introducing the system laid down in my tactics. Indeed, my friend, I have been fortunate in everything I have here undertaken. I am now fifth in rank as general ; and if my career be not ended by a fever or by half an ounce of lead, the possibilities are vast enough to satisfy the most ambitious. Two or three years of toil, and then, my friend, you must promise to visit me in Paris; and there we will discuss the question whether we are to dine together * in Europe or in America. Oh! my dearest F——, why have I wasted my years in such a manner! Two years of work—if one is not afraid of toil and danger—can make a man successful. Experience has convinced me of this; nor can I forgive myself for my past indolence.

What a beautiful, what a happy country this is! Without kings, without prelates, without blood-sucking farmer-generals,† and without idle barons! Here everybody is prosperous. Poverty is an unknown evil. Indeed, I should become too prolix were I to give you an account of the prosperity and happiness of these people.‡ The account of them by Abbé

---

* i.e., be associated together.

† *In verbis simus faciles, etc.* When Brutus freed Rome from kingly rule the Patricians spoke much of freedom, and meanwhile rode almost rough-shod over the Plebeians who had been released from the yoke. Again, under the Protector Cromwell many—especially gentlemen of the army—sang songs of praise that the king was no more. It is true that the word "farmer-general" has always been unknown in North America; but by what name shall we call those gentlemen who, since the year 1774, yearly take large sums (under threat of punishment by fire and sword) from the inhabitants for the purpose of continuing the war?—*Note by Schlözer.*

‡ All Europeans who have visited America during the

Reynal is not entirely accurate, but it is the best. Read it and judge for yourself.

But enough of myself and my new Fatherland. How are you, my friend, and how is our most serene sovereign? Please hand the enclosed to the best of princes, with the assurances of my most submissive respect. My happiness will only be complete when I hear that he has received convincing proofs of the intensity of my gratitude. My many duties and the uncertainty of the ocean have hitherto prevented my doing so. Before leaving Philadelphia, however, I requested a certain Mr. Robert Morris to procure a complete collection of North American trees (of which there are some 320 different varieties), and to send three or four specimens of each kind to the care of M. Gerard in Paris next fall. M. Gerard has promised to send the trees at my cost to Strasburg, at the same time notifying his serene highness the prince. Mr. Morris procured a similar collection this spring for the King of France. The Garden of Pheas-

---

present war unite in speaking of the wonderful prosperity of that country, which seems to strike the eye at a glance. This prosperity, admitted by both sides, has either begun since the rebellion of 1774,—a proposition which no one, in the very nature of things, can maintain, since a poverty-stricken people require a generation under the wisest of governments to become prosperous,—or the accounts must have been written at a previous period when North America was under British rule. That rule, therefore, could not have been either oppressive or tyrannical.—*Note by Schlözer.*

ants is the best place for this collection. Nothing
excepting the uncertainties of navigation will prevent
me at this or some future time from tendering my
respectful acknowledgments to the Princess and the
Princess von F—— in the way of West Indian goods.

And then, my friend, what shall I give *you?* and
what for H——? and also for ——? In truth, I
still have some acknowledgments to make before
closing my letter. How is Fr——? Is he married?
Is he happy? If not, let him come here, for I can
now reward his services. In case he should conclude
to do so, send me word speedily, and I will forward
his travelling expenses to Strasburg.

I wrote you that I would give Schleitheim employment here, although it is difficult to get along in
the service without a knowledge of English. I have
now thoroughly mastered that language, so that I
can write and speak of anything I wish; and I have
even written my " Tactics" in English.* Inasmuch as

---

* " In the autumn of 1780," says " Appleton's American
Biographical Cyclopædia," " Steuben published a Manual for
the army, furnished with diagrams to explain his rules. It
was entitled 'Regulations for the Order and Discipline of
the Troops of the United States.' Each chapter was written
first in poor German, then translated into poor French,
then put into good French, and lastly into good English, in
which last condition it was entirely unintelligible to Steuben. It nevertheless served its purpose, became the law and
guide of the army, and even after the war was adopted by
several of the States."

The above quotation, it will be seen from Steuben's letter,

Schleitheim did not arrive here, and as I have received no word from you since I wrote you about him, I infer that you have either failed to receive my letter, or that he has been provided for in another way. Moreover, I must candidly admit to you that six foreign officers cause more trouble to me here than two hundred American ones ; and indeed most of the foreigners have so utterly lost their credit, that it is daily becoming more difficult to employ foreign officers. A large number of German barons and French marquises have already sailed away ;* and I am

contains two grave errors: 1st. The Manual was published in 1779; and, 2d, so far from its being unintelligible to Steuben in English, he expressly says he had written it himself in that language. The quotation also, it seems to me, contains a slur upon Steuben, by intimating that it was first written in " poor German "—Steuben's own mother-tongue. This is tantamount to saying that Steuben was illiterate, which certainly was not the case : on the contrary, it was far otherwise. It is surprising, also, that Kapp (a conscientious and able historian) in his "Life of Baron Steuben" falls into one of these errors. Speaking of the Manual, he says: " It was afterward written in good English by Captain Walker; and when it was completed Steuben did not understand a word of it himself, from his ignorance of the English language"! I say "surprising ;" because Kapp, whom personally I knew well, was one of the most kind-hearted and genial of men, and would not willingly have done injustice to a human being, no matter how lowly his station.

* The reader will recall the letter from Boston, in which the writer says that " thirty-one French officers are to sail shortly back to France."

always nervous and apprehensive when a baron or a marquis announces himself. While here we are in a republic; and Mr. Baron does not count a farthing more than Mister Jacob or Mister Peter. Indeed, German and French noses can hardly accustom themselves to such a state of things ! Our general of artillery, for instance, was a bookbinder in Boston.* He is a worthy man, thoroughly understands his trade, and fills his present position with much credit.

Baron von Kalbe and myself are now the only foreign generals in the United States service ; and Kalbe, who has an income of over 30,000 livres in France, will resign at the end of this campaign.†

Finally, my friend, I will only state to you my prospects and then close my letter. I will finish the war here, or it will finish me. Without doubt England, at the utmost, can continue the game but two years longer. It will then be my care to put the army and the militia in the thirteen provinces on a uniform and solid footing; and this having been accomplished, I shall render an account to Congress as to what we owe each other. My ability to keep up my appointments on 16,400 livres is assured to me for life. Congress has promised me, not gifts, but a landed estate either in New Jersey or Pennsylvania, two of the best

---

* General Knox.

† Kalbe was recently (16th Aug. 1780) killed in the engagement at Camden. He was wounded, captured, and died.— *Note by Schlözer.*

provinces.* A considerable pension from France, after the (successful) termination of the war, was pledged to me by the French Court before my departure for America; besides which, I can depend upon receiving a substantial gratuity especially from the thirteen provinces. To acquire all this requires on my part only three years, at the farthest, of life, health, steadfastness of purpose and courage. The first two conditions do not depend upon me : the last two are within my power and control. And then, my friend, when these have been fulfilled! *Then* shall I see you in Europe ; and *then* we can talk the matter over, and decide whether you shall in future dine with me in Paris or Philadelphia!

Believe me, my friend, this globe of ours is not so large as we imagine it! An ant does not deserve its food if it is too lazy to seek it at the other side of its hill; and I have already wasted fourteen years of my life. Now, is Canada my hunting-lodge ; Georgia my

---

* "After the war Congress, with its usual vacillating course, refused to fulfil its contract with Steuben to pay him for his services, but he was given grants of land in Virginia, Pennsylvania, and New Jersey. The latter he declined to accept when he found it consisted of the confiscated estates of an old Tory who would be left destitute, and, in the kindness of his heart, he interceded for him. He was also given a whole township near Utica, N. Y., and after seven years' delay Congress at length allowed him a pension of $2400." He retired to this land, and, clearing off 60 acres, built a log-house in which he lived until his death, which occurred on the 22d Nov. 1795.

country-seat ; and this strip of land the eighth of the world. At each of these extreme ends an order signed by me will be executed. This is somewhat flattering to an ambitious man ; and you can, therefore, recognize your friend !

When you write to me, my best of friends, address your letters to the care of M. Gerard at Versailles, through whose agency I shall more securely receive them. This is his address : "*M. Gerard, Conseiller des Affaires Étrangers* à Versailles." And here is mine :

" To His Excellence, the honorable Baron of Steuben, Inspector-General and Major-General of the Armies of the United States in North America."

Have the kindness, my friend, to send the worthy General R——d an abstract of my letter. My many engagements prevent me from writing to all the people whom I esteem and honor. Sp—— is to be classed with those people. Let him know of my present circumstances; for I am certain they will interest him. Should General R——, or any other of my friends, know of any officers or other persons who would like to try their luck in this part of the world, a line written by them to me will be sufficient by them to secure my very best endeavors to promote their welfare.

Farewell ; and long and happily may you live, my dearest friend ! Let me soon hear from you ; and I remain, with the sincerest friendship,

Yours, most truly,
STEUBEN.

APPENDIX.

The following sketch of the Récollets and their convent is condensed from an address on the English cathedral of Quebec, recently delivered before the "Historical Society" of that city by its accomplished librarian, Mr. F. C. Würtele:

The mendicant order of friars called Franciscans was founded in Spain, in the year 1208, by St. Francis d'Assisi, and subsequently were introduced into France by St. Louis of Gonzaga. They were also called "Récollets," from the Latin word *Recollectus*, signifying "meditation" and also "gathering." Their chief works were teaching, nursing the sick, and ministering to the poor, whose wants they supplied out of the donations and alms which they received. In fact, their livelihood was obtained entirely by begging, performed by the "Frères Mineurs;" and so highly were they esteemed and beloved in old Canada, that the *habitans* would always transport free of charge the results of their begging expeditions from village to village, and finally to the convent in Quebec. The boatmen, also, invariably were pleased to ferry them free across the St. Lawrence. In 1614, four Récollets were chosen as missionaries to Canada, namely: Fathers Denis Jamay, the superior; Jean D'Olbeau, Joseph LeCaron, and Brother Pacifique Duplessis. They assembled at Rouen in March, 1615, and sailed from

Honfleur on the 24th April, arriving at Tadousac on the 25th May, and proceeding thence to Quebec. A temporary chapel and house were erected near the "Abitation," now the site of the Church of Notre-Dame des Victoires.

This was the first church erected in the French possessions in North America. The convent was first completed, but the church was not ready for consecration until 25th May, 1621, and was named Notre-Dame des Anges. Père LeClerq narrates that they still retained the house and chapel erected in 1615, in the lower town of Quebec, and used them as Hospice and "Chapelle succursale." The establishment on the St. Charles was strongly built and of a semi-military character, fitted with bastions and surrounded with palisades, in order to guard against the raids of the Indians. In fact the building was hardly completed when the friars repulsed a serious attack of the Iroquois.

In 1677, Governor Frontenac built for them, at his own expense, a large convent, to which, in 1678, a chapel and sacristy were added. The Récollets, however, had not been ten years in possession of their convent when they wished to establish themselves in the Upper Town of Quebec, and on the 8th May, 1681, they obtained from the king an emplacement called the "Senechaussée" or "Seneschal's Jurisdiction," between Garden, St. Anne, and St. Louis streets, on which they built by degrees a convent and church.

At the siege of Quebec, in 1759, the Récollet buildings were considerably damaged by the fire of the British; and this calamity, together with the fall of Quebec, having rendered homeless the few friars that remained, they dispersed. From this time the number of Récollets diminished year by year, so that their convent was too large for them, but in 1776 the unoccupied portion was used as a jail for political offenders, and the American prisoners taken in Montgomery's fatal attack on Quebec, 31st December of that year, were there locked up.

The Récollects were most liberal towards other religious denominations, for it is recorded in the *Quebec Gazette* of Thursday, 21st May, 1767, that : "On Sunday next, divine service, according to the use of the Church of England, will be at the Récollets' church and continue for the summer season, beginning soon after eleven. The drum will beat each Sunday soon after half an hour past ten, and the Récollets' bell will ring, to give notice of the English service, the instant their own is ended."

The Récollet convent and church were again burned on the 6th of September, 1796; and after the fire the Government took possession of the property and razed the ruins. Part of the foundation wall could till lately be seen in the roadway between the Cathedral and Place d'Armes near the crossing. That portion of it now surrounded by a stone wall forms the English Cathedral " *Close.*"

INDEX.

ERRATA.

Pages 13, 41. For " Bec Island," read " Bic Island."

Page 48. For " Isle au Custus," read " Isle au Castor."

Page 71, 6th line from bottom. For " *Fêtes*" read "*Têtes.*"

Page 84, last line of note. For "New Hampshire" read " New York."

Page 94. 8th line from top, for "any" read "every."

Page 128, note. For " Gen. I. Watts de Peyster" read " J. Watts de Peyster."

Page 199, 5th line from bottom. For "pear" read "apple."

Page 218, 1st line of note. Omit " Jr." after " J. G. Rosengarten."

Page 245, note. For " Rogers " read " Rodgers. "